Two Wheels on Two Reels

A History of Biker Movies

By Mike Seate

Whitehorse Press
North Conway, New Hampshire

Cover photo and About the Author photo by Kim Love
Back cover photo by Duane Rieder Photography

We recognize that some words, model names and designations
mentioned herein are the property of the trademark holder. We
use them for identification purposes only.

Whitehorse Press is a trademark of Kennedy Associates.

Whitehorse Press books are also available at discounts in bulk
quantity for sales and promotional use. For details about
special sales or for a catalog of motorcycling books and videos,
write to the publisher:

Whitehorse Press
P.O. Box 60
North Conway, New Hampshire 03860-0060
Phone: 603-356-6556 or 800-531-1133
E-mail: Orders@WhitehorsePress.com
Internet: www.WhitehorsePress.com

ISBN 1-884313-25-6

5   4   3   2   1

Printed in the United States of America

Contents

To my friend, Charlie Humphrey, for believing in my writing before I did, and to my wife Kim, for keeping me going.

Introduction

Like most Americans growing up during the 1960s and 70s, my first impressions of bikers came from watching motorcycle movies. Because the biker lifestyle is a relatively new tradition, it has little in the way of folklore to hand down from generation to generation.

Until the recent proliferation of motorcycling lifestyle magazines, biker movies provided the outside world—or, to borrow lingo from biker movies themselves, "straights" and "citizens,"—with their only glimpse of the biker's world. To view a motorcyclist's mysterious and sometimes dangerous lifestyle, you could either take a movie director's word for it, or visit your local biker bar.

Most people chose the former.

So with the sensational eye of Hollywood as our guide, we learned about bikes and bikers from drive-in theaters and late-night television—and not from a grizzled uncle who had ridden with an outlaw gang, popped pills with Hunter Thompson, and endured knife-fights in Deadwood saloons. It was here that we learned the rules: that any *real* biker would rather die than give up his chopper; that Hondas aren't as cool as Harleys; that booze and broads are as important as the bike itself.

A talk with any number of motorcycle enthusiasts will reveal that biker movies, however dubious their content, profoundly influenced their decision to start riding.

Filmmakers only began to realize the box office potential of bikers after the public tired of cowboys and Indians in the Western genre in the mid-1960s. The much-publicized newspaper stories about gangs of drug- and speed-crazed bikers marauding across middle America in search of thrills and "whatever comes our way," to paraphrase Steppenwolf, was a godsend for filmmakers eager to please a public who needed clearly delineated good guys and bad guys. They also needed sex, action, and heady images of anti-establishment rebellion, elements that dramatizations of the biker lifestyle had in excess.

In time, biker movies practically killed the Western, relegating Hop-A-Long Cassidy to the close-out bin of popular culture and forever enshrining the wild, bearded motorcycle hoodlum in the world's memory.

Unfortunately, Hollywood's exploitation of the motorcycle outlaw proved to be a sword that cut both ways for motorcyclists: the films undeniably raised awareness of motorcycles, but did so at a price. Most motorcyclists at the time felt the popular image of drugged-out chopper riders had little to do with their riding experiences, and worse, much of the public began seeing everyone on two wheels through the same nefarious prism.

Whatever their motivations, it's no surprise that filmmakers have been attracted to motorcycling as a catalyst for their movies. The raw, aesthetic appeal and patent thrill embodied by two-wheeled travel and racing has an inherent magnetism, a look-at-me element that has caught the eye of filmmakers since the Marx Brothers first piled into an old Indian Scout sidecar rig for a sight gag in *Duck Soup*. Motorcycles are flawless props for directors in need of an instant boost of speed and excitement, and their flash and noise are foolproof devices when a filmmaker wants to draw a disinterested audience's gaze from their yawning popcorn bowls.

In films as diverse as the post-apocalyptic gang wars of the Japanese animation epic *Akira*, to the hokey, action-chase potboiler *Fled*, the primary role of the motorcycle has been to excite moviegoers where special effects, plot twists, and other devices have failed.

However mixed the results or sincere the efforts to bring motorcycling to life on screen, biker movies have earned a permanent place in the film and pop culture canon. This book discusses not only the impact these films have had on motorcyclists, but also examines the world's perception of bikers as well. In no way is this book intended to serve as an encyclopedia of biker films, as many of the movies produced during the most prolific period of the mid-to-late 1960s have vanished, along with their casts, into the proverbial B-movie sunset.

Some would say this is for the better.

There have been few serious attempts to chronicle biker movies, mainly, I suspect, because the studios that produced them did so with only minimal care. Production values were often thrown out along with pretensions of accuracy and fairness. As *Pittsburgh Press* film critic Ed Blank once observed, "Of course all the biker movies were poorly done. If they looked like *Gone With The Wind* no bikers would have gone to see them."

The actors who starred in them—or at least those who went on to star in other films—tend to downplay their appearances in biker movies, or selectively omit these films from their resumes. Robert Redford, for example, fleshed out his sociopathic motorcycle racer in director Sidney J. Furie's *Little Fauss and Big Halsy* so well that the actor has publicly denounced the movie and his part in it.

For the most part, it was only select members of the moviegoing audience who saw biker movies as anything more than disposable summer fun.

Syndicated film critic Roger Ebert once told an interviewer that he never knew who the intended audience was for the low-budget, drive-in biker movies of the 1960s, but admitted to having seen nearly all of them at a second-run Chicago movie house as a teen. The popularity of biker movies, whether in revivals at art houses, on late night cable television, or from brisk video sales, lends Ebert's candor an undeniable element of truth—they were, and remain, guilty pleasures.

Without their newfound cult status, even fewer biker movies would have been transferred to video and been made available to a second generation of fans.

However unrealistic and outdated the films could be (and often still are), they manage, through blatant emulation, secondhand experience, and oftentimes clumsy attempts by real bikers acting and serving as technical consultants, to create a visual and historical record of the world's motorcycling subcultures. The result is a lifestyle which has grown by remarkable lengths, not only in its native United States, but across the globe in places as remote as war-scarred Bosnia and as unlikely as Moscow.

From Brando's thick-lipped mutterings in Stanley Kramer's *The Wild One*, to the revisionist biker-as-hero sagas of later films like *Mask*, biker movies, with their portrayals of motorcyclists as rebels, heroes, anti-heroes and above all, outsiders, have provided a fascinating chronicle into how the world perceives rebellion, its youth, and the need, to quote Peter Fonda in *The Wild Angels*, "To be free, to ride our machines without being hassled by the man. And, to get loaded."

—Mike Seate, Pittsburgh, June, 2000

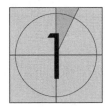

Origins of the Wild Ones

Imagine it's 1954 and you've just picked up the kids for a night at the local drive-in. Earlier this year your family delighted in watching Gregory Peck romance a lithe Audrey Hepburn in director William Wyler's storybook romantic comedy *Roman Holiday.* But tonight the drive-in is screening something called *The Wild One,* a movie you've heard has something to do with people traveling by motorcycle.

Few people in the audiences could have been prepared for what they saw during the brief, 79-minute drama. The movie contained no profanity and only the vaguest of references to sex, but with its casual violence and near-total refusal to delineate a hero or authority figure, *The Wild One* starring Marlon Brando as Johnny, Lee Marvin as rival gang leader "Chino," and a sad-eyed Mary Murphy as Kathie, broke nearly every rule in the American movie book.

You would have had to look deep and hard at the pantheon of limited-release, B-grade films of the 1950s to find another movie where the town cop was a cowardly alcoholic and the most likable character a pouty delinquent with a winning smile.

Nearly 60 years and dozens of sordid chopper-operas from American International Pictures later, its easy to forget that *The Wild One,* which many critics have credited as the first real motorcycle film, was as groundbreaking and alarming in its day as the controversial rap-music film *Menace 2 Society* was to modern audiences.

Just how alarming was it? Well, consider that *The Wild One* was banned outright in the UK for 12 years after its initial release. In Britain at the time, censors feared the movie would inspire anti-social behavior in teens. Sure, there were other youth rebellion films released prior to *The Wild One,* but sophomoric efforts like *Devil on Wheels* (1947), with rapidly-maturing child star Mickey Rooney in the lead, played more like feature-length driver-training films than serious studies of the darker side of youth.

Part of the timeless appeal of *The Wild One* is due to director Laszlo Benedek's ability to capture the opening spasms of the postwar youth rebellion movement, with scenes that would forever change pop culture and American society in general. In a few years, films focusing on the antics of both juvenile and seasoned delinquents, were to become as common as greasy hair at an Elvis concert. But Benedek did it first, and nearly every domestic motorcycle film made after *The Wild One* is indebted to his work in one way or another.

While essentially a motorcycle film, *The Wild One* explored more than just biker angst; there was an underlying theme of postwar discontent

Still considered the seminal biker movie, *The Wild One* cemented into the public consciousness the marauding motorcycle gang. A young Marlon Brando was equally memorable as the quintessential rebellious-but-thoughtful leader, Johnny. (Columbia Pictures)

handy excuse to stave off the inevitability of marriage, mortgage, and diaper pail.

While post-war anguish was a common malady, few Hollywood films dared to address what many Americans were already aware of: WWII may have ended on the battlefields in August of '45, but the wounds would take much longer to heal.

Director William Wyler's *The Best Years of Our Lives* (1946), a timely post-war drama about a maladjusted crew of returning veterans was one of the few films to take an honest look at problems the War Department would have rather ignored. With the war over, the former pilots, seamen, and soldiers in Wyler's film ended up immersing themselves in either rivers of booze or long days of self-loathing. It wasn't exactly as enjoyable as the Andy Griffith/Don Knotts military comedy *No Time For Sergeants* (1958), but *Best Years* garnered seven Academy Awards for its heartfelt realism.

In a way, *The Wild One* was a continuation of sorts of Wyler's theme of post-war discontent. References to WWII or any current events are glaringly omitted from *The Wild One*, but the film's characters are clearly derived from this generation of veterans.

Benedek's story is actually a fictionalized, and some would say sensationalized, account of a drunken weekend riot that occurred at the annual 4th of July motorcycle races in sleepy Hollister, California back in 1947. To create the final screenplay, this real-life event was combined with elements from *Cyclists Raid* a scintillating piece of fiction from writer Frank Rooney published in the January, 1951 issue of *Harper's Magazine*.

During pre-production, the filmmakers conducted dozens of interviews with nomad bikers from California. These taped interviews helped build authentic characterizations in scenes where the gang members would fight each other like

that was familiar to most motorcyclists riding at the time. The many restless WWII veterans taking to America's highways on hopped-up motorcycles saw the two-wheeler as both cheap transportation and also a primitive form of therapy. In a protracted conflict which saw some 7 million Americans don uniforms, the uneasy transition from the stresses of war to the relative prosperity and gentility of peacetime life was one of the great under-reported social crises of the century.

At the core of this new group of wandering, rootless Americans were the motorcyclists who took to the roads in search of personal freedom. Many veterans who felt that civilian life was too confining found that motorcycles could help recreate some of the excitement and adrenaline rush of the war years. Bikes also provided a crazed dogs one moment, only to rejoin to the bar, arm-in-arm, minutes later. Riding motorcycles into bars, racing on public streets, and the peculiar outlaw biker habit of dressing up in costume to shock the "citizens" (evident when a member of Marvin's Beetles tugs on his sizable beard only to reveal the face shrubbery is attached to his hat with a pair of rubber bands) were all lifted from biker lore in the 1950s.

Because the early bike gangs were nearly all comprised of former servicemen, the gangs in *The Wild One*, Brando's Black Rebels and Lee Marvin's rag-tag gang the Beetles, both followed an almost military template. Both groups were fiercely loyal to their respective leaders much like a fighter squadron or infantry platoon. And once the fists had flown and the groups were united by a common adversary—in this case a town full of uptight citizens—their differences were cast aside like an empty beer bottle.

Having been produced in the early 1950s when rock and roll, or more accurately, rhythm and blues music was still largely relegated to black audiences, *The Wild One's* bikers appeared even more outlandish for speaking an odd mix of ghetto slang and be-bop jazz dialect (plenty of "Daddy-O's" and "slap me some skin, man," are tossed about). Today's viewers can barely imagine how troubling these gangs of hopped-up city boys on motorcycles, listening to wild jungle music, must have seemed in middle America.

Besides the rusty-looking Harley Flathead ridden by Marvin's Chino, most of the motorcycles in *The Wild One* are bone-stock machines, as the full customizing movement was still in its infancy at the time of production. Some 15 years later when William Smith and Dennis Hopper were the cinema's principal motorcycling heavies, the customized chopper would become as central to

After the 1954 release of *The Wild One*, bikers emulated Marlon Brando's Johnny in fashion and spirit. In the 1970s, outlaw biker gangs would again be inspired by a Brando role: the crafty, stoic, Mafia crime boss from Francis Ford Coppola's *The Godfather*. (Columbia Pictures)

biker movies as the plot itself. Here, the rather conservative Triumphs and Matchless twins favored by the Black Rebels are among the artifacts that make *The Wild One* look dated.

The movie opens with Brando's gang interrupting a sanctioned oval-track race. When they're run off the course by the cops, they rejoin to a small town for a few beers. There, the Black Rebels run into Kathie working in the town's small café. As biker movie women would do for decades, Kathie attracts Johnny's eye despite her squareness. But while Kathie and Johnny circle each other warily, the gang also has the misfortune to run into Johnny's arch-rival Chino.

After clearing up past differences with a public brawl which lands Chino in jail, both gangs decide to hang around the one-horse town for reasons never made entirely clear. Bored, drunk, and restless, the two gangs begin to "terrorize" the townsfolk with a series of stunts and pranks that seem mild compared to the Spring Break antics of your average college fraternity. A few hair dryers are misused as hats, quite a few beers are consumed, and a few bikers dance drunkenly in the streets, but that's about it for anti-social behavior.

By the film's end, the townspeople find enough courage to eject the biker gangs just as the street party is reaching its apex. Though Brando is punched out by a feeble crew of vigilantes and his Triumph Thunderbird veers out of control and fatally injures an elderly bystander, there's never much of a sense of menace to the proceedings.

For instance, the town's pair of old maids seem genuinely pleased with the attentions of so many rugged, young male admirers and there are many deliberate shots of the cash register in the village tavern repeatedly ringing up the biker's dollars.

In British sociologist-turned-Hell's Angel Maz Harris' 1985 biographical novel *Biker: Birth of a Modern-Day Outlaw,* Harris includes an interview with *Wild One* producer Stanley Kramer. The producer reveals insights into the stifling political and social climate in which the film was made. According to Kramer, in the film's original ending, the townspeople decline to press charges against the two gangs because of how much money the bikers had pumped into the town's coffers. Reflecting the mood of many merchants during the actual Hollister melee, Kramer culled the scene from the interviews he'd conducted with actual participants in the Hollister event. But at the height of the McCarthy era, when political moralizing had become a national pastime, film industry censors nullified that ending, concerned that it could be interpreted as an anti-American indictment of capitalism.

Instead, the film closes with Johnny escaping prosecution when police learn that his motorcycle hit a pedestrian during the melee because he was struck by a tire iron thrown by the crowds of vigilantes. Johnny returns just before the closing credits to leave his stolen racing trophy with barmaid Kathie as an act of contrition. Whether audiences realized a patently moralistic ending had been tacked on to an otherwise honest look at the dollar's ability to heal all wounds didn't much matter: *The Wild One* had ridden through town via the country's movie screens. Black leather and motorcycles would never be viewed in quite the same way.

The film was a first in many ways. It introduced the formula of the cycle gang invading and terrorizing the small provincial town. This formula would eventually provide an easy setting for any biker movie director lacking imagination. Brando, who would go on to film superstardom for his work in Tennessee William's *A Streetcar Named Desire* and much later, Francis Ford Coppola's film adaptation of Mario Puzo's *The Godfather,* propagated the myth of the outlaw biker with the heart of gold, a character we'd see much more of in the 1980s and beyond. And almost unintentionally, *The Wild One* helped make black leather jackets, a garment traditionally associated with the patriotic dash of the fighter pilot, a universally recognized icon of anti-social behavior.

Admittedly, this is a tall order for a single film to encompass, particularly one which didn't exactly light fires of inspiration under any of the day's critics. Most critics were either turned off by the film's nihilism or saw the cycle gangs as an affront to all things decent. The wholesale denouncement of *The Wild One* speaks volumes about why no major Hollywood studio would venture back into the world of biker gangs for over ten years. Bikers, on the other hand, loved it. Even today, when *The Wild One* is shown at revival houses or at biker rallies, crowds cheer and howl when the film's police chief, played by stone-faced Jay C. Flippen barks the foreboding order: "That's it: round up everybody on a motorsickle!" How prophetic.

Or, take for example a story recounted by writer Hunter S. Thompson in his 1966 study of outlaw biker gangs, *Hell's Angels.* In the year Thompson spent drinking with and writing about the West Coast's outlaw gangs, he came across one Frank Sadilek, a retired chapter president of the notorious San Francisco chapter of the Hell's Angels. Sadilek idolized, or better yet, revered Marvin's moldy, beer-addled Chino so much, the real-life outlaw paid a visit to the Hollywood studio where *The Wild One* had been produced and pestered the costume department to let him purchase the very blue and yellow striped sweatshirt Marvin had worn during filming. Sadilek, who was president of the gang from 1955 to 1962, reportedly wore the shirt until it became nothing more than a waistcoat of tattered, beer-soaked threads. Somehow, Marvin's rather goofy-looking sweater, a garment that wouldn't have looked out of place on a character from Charles Schultz' "Peanuts," had became an outlaw biker fashion staple. The enduring legacy of *The Wild One* lives on with copies of Lee Marvin's sweater

"What are you rebelling against?"
"What have you got?"
Johnny (Marlon Brando)
The Wild One

available through ads in biker lifestyle publications, and posters of a leather-jacketed Brando still popular sellers in college campus bookstores.

The Wild One did plenty to instill in the public a fear of, or at least fascination with, motorcyclists, but however legendary Johnny had become, he was an image nightmare for the majority of law-abiding bike riders. In countless mainstream magazine articles, the thuggery and mischief of *The Wild One* was the worst public relations mishap ever to befall two-wheeled transportation. Everyday motorcycle enthusiasts and serious competition riders alike rankled at the thought of being lumped together by a distrustful public with the drunken yobbos, chopper riders, and miscreants depicted in the 1954 film. Jack Hall, a veteran motorcycle shop owner from Pennsylvania recalls going to see *The Wild One* with his friends when it premiered at Pittsburgh's Art Cinema, a B-movie venue that doubled as the city's top burlesque house. Hall said the film had a polarizing effect on his group of riders, with "one half cheering from the balcony" during the movie's rowdier scenes, while another group sat in silence, almost shamefaced. "Right away, some of our guys wanted to imitate Brando, walking like he did and trying to act super-cool. There were some guys who only thought about what the cops or their next-door neighbors would think after a movie like that," said Hall. Hall said police harassment of bikers didn't immediately escalate in the wake of *The Wild One's* release, but corresponding news stories about cycling riots and drunken biker rampages began to take their toll by the late 1950s. Bosses in some of Pittsburgh's steel plants where Hall and his friends worked occasionally forbade employees from riding motorcycles to work. Hall also recalled how neighbors and relatives frequently assumed "that you're some kind of badass or hood just because you ride a sickle."

And like today's gangsta rap music and films, a public outcry against screening *The Wild One* was launched (unsuccessfully) by religious and parent's groups in Cincinnati, Ohio and Miami,

Florida in the summer of 1954. Newspaper headlines began referring to youthful hoodlums, whether astride motorcycles or not, as "Brandos" in homage to a role the actor himself almost immediately dismissed as insignificant.

Hall's experience was not radically different from that of thousands of bikers across the country. After the Hollister riot, the American Motorcyclist Association issued a now-infamous statement chastising the "one percent of motorcyclists" responsible for the problems that characterized the 1947 Hollister rally. In provocation, members of some of the rowdier motorcycle clubs—first in Southern California and soon thereafter, the world—adopted the AMA's dismissal of them as a badge of honor, deeming themselves "One Percenters." The nefarious diamond-shaped patch has since become as synonymous with outlaw culture as the FBI's Most Wanted poster. In many ways, the One Percenter image still plays on fears introduced to the public through the same events that spawned Kramer's film some 60 years ago.

Though not a biker movie, the 1950's second most notable youth rebellion flick, *Rebel Without A Cause* (1955), was released just one year after *The Wild One*, bringing further attention to this growing problem. *Rebel Without a Cause,* with an ensemble cast of future movie stars including James Dean, Sal Mineo, Natalie Wood, and Dennis Hopper, proved so compelling and provocative, its box-office and critical success eventually proved to Hollywood that stories of this type were capable of generating both headlines *and* receipts.

Rebel took on the conformity and dysfunction of the typical suburban family decades before Jerry Springer would make exploiting such people a daytime TV staple. These bored, thrill-seeking, upper-middle class teenagers were every successful parent's nightmare, proving that which side of the tracks kids came from had very little to do with how long a teenager stayed out of trouble. Bent on self-destruction, Dean's crew—who favored hot-rod cars instead of motorcycles—eventually tear themselves and the facade of suburban propriety to shreds. If *The Wild One* revealed how potentially unsafe the country's backroads were, *Rebel Without A Cause* seemed to warn parents to look for the enemy under their own roof.

However popular and groundbreaking *The Wild One* and *Rebel* proved to be, it took film studios a few years to realize the box office potential of further exploiting youth rebellion. There were very few movies about angry, wayward youth made in the next three years—with the exception of the excellent *Blackboard Jungle* (1955)—a lull that in today's terms would be considered a lifetime.

But once the gears got rolling, Hollywood's low budget film studios cranked out a burgeoning roster of teen exploitation movies. Motorcycles, with their innate ability to instill fear into the average citizen were showing up with increasing regularity. In a half-hearted attempt to recreate some of the cultural climate surrounding *The Wild One*, prolific B-movie maven Samuel Z. Arkoff released *Motorcycle Gang* in 1958. Starring none other than former *Our Gang* star Carl "Alfalfa" Sweitzer as "Speed," this clumsy teen exploitation classic actually used a slightly altered script from *Dragstrip Girl* which director Edward L. Cahn had finished only months before.

Both films, with their predictable appeals for kids to avoid trouble, play like one-act dramas staged in the cellar of a local church. *Motorcycle Gang's* main characters are the Skyriders, a group of motorcyclists so dedicated to clean, disciplined living that their biggest transgression involved driving 90 mph on public streets. Blatting around on an assortment of British twins and Harleys, the Skyriders are preoccupied with practicing for the upcoming Pacific Motorcycle Championships Race. That, and exchanging some of the corniest come-on lines this side of a John Holmes movie. "What have you been smoking, baby? Salmon?" asks Terry Lindsay (Ann Nyland) of Nick (John Ashley). "I hope I live long enough to be one of your pall bearers," quips another actor. Where *The Wild One* presented bikers in a moody, film noir cover of darkness, the low-budget *Motorcycle Gang*, is filmed almost entirely in the bright West Coast sunshine: the results are a gang epic that is seldom more disturbing than being stuck in a slow line at Disneyland.

Our hero Randy (played with plenty of boy-next-door charm by Steve Terrell) is a reformed delinquent who is single-mindedly determined to win the approaching 100-mile cross-country race. His former partner in crime, Nick, however, has other ideas. Like Chino, Nick is upset that the once wild and woolly gang has split up. Unless Randy denounces clean living and competition riding, well, there's going to be trouble. The ensuing 78 minutes are a hilarious display of stagey fist fights, thwarted innuendoes, and obviously faked riding sequences where the Skyriders and their rivals pose on bikes in front of moving backdrops. Arkoff diffuses the melodrama with plenty of slapstick comedy; each heavy character is offset by a grinning, wisecracking opposite.

Nick and Randy are intent on proving who's more deserving of Terry's affections by challenging each other to a series of particularly bone-jarring off-road races. It's telling of the times that, a scant eight years later, movie motorcycle gangs would have simply shared the woman and been too stoned to consider anything as physically demanding as an off-road race on a street bike.

Motorcycle Gang, originally titled *Motorcycle Girl*, was released as one of American International Picture's drive-in double-features, playing alongside *Sorority Girl*, which was billed as a tell-all expose of collegiate decadence. It was one of the first biker movies to follow in *The Wild One's* wake, and it conformed to that film's template faithfully. *Motorcycle Gang* copied *The Wild One's* moral struggles and crazy-cool dialogue. It also took great pains to reveal that some outlaws have hearts of gold. Terrell's Randy, for instance, only wants to stay clean so he can race. Getting involved with his old crowd would mean violating his court-ordered probation, which he received after a fatal traffic accident where he and Nick killed an elderly pedestrian. "Nick wants the good old days when every kid on a motorcycle was considered a criminal with a gun," observes the club's adult leader, police Lt. Joe Watson, played by veteran actor Russ Bender.

Being unfamiliar with motorcycles didn't stop some actors and actresses from seeking roles in biker movies. Here, director Jack Cardiff helps Marianne Faithful dismount Alan Delon's Norton Atlas on the set of *Girl on a Motorcycle*. (Mid Atlantic/Ares Productions)

The movie benefited from an unexpected public relations windfall when a pair of Philadelphia teenagers on their way to see *Motorcycle Gang* stole a car and were involved in a fatal hit-and-run accident with a pedestrian, just as the film's main characters had been. *The Philadelphia Inquirer* ran the story on its front page, indelibly linking it with Arkoff's otherwise forgettable film. As a result, box-office receipts soared briefly since no self-respecting rebellious teen could pass up a movie that could generate this kind of audience reaction.

Despite its low budget, *Motorcycle Gang* does contain a few surprisingly good riding sequences. These are interspersed with several minutes of stock footage from vintage off-road races held on the West Coast. There's also an extremely funny

Low budgets for biker movies often meant filming "road" sequences indoors. Here, *Motorcycle Gang* star Anne Neyland simulates a highway blast in front of a movie screen. (American International Pictures)

sequence where Nick's gang "menaces" the population of a small town—all six townspeople—by forcing them to watch an improvised motorcycle stunt show. Good eventually conquers evil, with Nick headed back to jail, and Randy making off with Nyland's Terry, the trophy blonde. "These guys aren't club members. They're alley cats on motorcycles," Lt. Watson explains to the townspeople as he leads the defeated outlaws away, perhaps the first film attempt to delineate outlaw bikers from motorcycling's mainstream.

For all its moral posturing and overwrought violence, *Motorcycle Gang* was never considered a "serious" movie. Critics and audiences lumped it into the rest of A.I.P.'s teen exploitation films.

> "What have you been smoking, baby? Salmon?"
> Terry Lindsay (Ann Nyland)
> to Nick (John Ashley)
> *Motorcycle Gang*

Plot-wise, it was barely distinguishable from another A.I.P. release, 1958's *Dragstrip Riot*. In this trash classic, a gang of hot-rod racing "teens"—a relative term, as most of the actors featured in these films were long past the acne stage—run afoul of a small, but determined motorcycle gang.

By now, the black leather and DA haircuts had become standard issue for screen bikers. The motorcycles, too, were starting to reveal traits of the Bob Job customizing movement, with the front fenders of most of the Triumph twins and Harley-Davidson Flatheads and Knuckleheads having been removed.

Though *Dragstrip Riot* was billed with the tag line "Murder At 120 Miles Per Hour" the two

No screen biker was complete without a switchblade knife and a sneer to complement his black leather jacket as illustrated in the juvenile delinquent classic *Dragstrip Riot* (1958). (American International Pictures)

gangs seem to have more of a taste for staging sneering and wisecracking contests. The bikes do square off against the cars in some highly dramatic games of chicken, some even staged—as in *Motorcycle Gang*—along railroad trestles. And in a campy movie that heralded both the last screen work of *King Kong* star Fay Wray *and* the introduction of singer-actress Connie Stevens, the gang's incongruous use of spear guns during a drag race somehow doesn't seem so out of place.

As marginal as most of these movies were, (and for the most part, they were) A.I.P. was filling a void by releasing films that most mainstream studios wouldn't touch. There's little wonder why big studios steered clear of biker movies during most of the 1950s: there were Congressional hearings underway to establish blame for the country's growing number of juvenile criminals. Parent's groups established to protect the public's decency blamed rock and roll music, the ever-present Commie threat. During their all-consuming search for scapegoats, federal authorities in 1957 began to enforce strict censorship on comic books, targeting sexual imagery, anti-establishment messages, and violence. With so much pressure on society to clean up youth culture, film studios found biker gangs just too touchy an issue.

Even burgeoning television mostly ignored the biker lifestyle. One notable exception was a segment of the popular NBC TV show *The Twilight Zone*. Screenwriter and actor Rod Serling played on the Cold War fears of his viewers when he included a gang of leather-clad bikers in a 1964 episode titled *The Black Leather Jackets*. In this 20-minute vignette, a foursome of typically angry motorcycle riders move into a respectable suburban neighborhood where they hope to go unnoticed, even though they walk in lockstep and wear Lone Ranger masks around town.

Serling, always the clever social commentator, quickly establishes the suburban neighbors as

Though an avid motorcycle enthusiast in real life, Elvis Presley was only once to appear in film on a bike. In *Roustabout* (1964) the King of Rock and Roll is a wandering troubadour on a Honda 350 Superhawk—mounting Presley on a Harley in those times might have been too controversial. (Paramount Studios)

tribute to S&M bars and a rather fetishistic view of motorcycling is one of the strangest takes on biking ever to reach the screen.

Released to almost immediate acclaim on the art house circuit, Anger's film is an uneven montage of well-oiled bodybuilders, static shots of full-dressed Harley touring bikes (which would later become something of an icon in the gay community) and disturbing shots of various religious artifacts.

Scorpio Rising was probably a source of much confusion and embarrassment to any straight biker who mistakenly wandered into a screening expecting to see a righteous biker flick about screwing on the throttle and hangin' with the bros. But as seen in the short's closing segments, the cult of the motorcycle obviously had adherents in the seamy underworld of S&M bars and dominance parlors. The mind boggles imagining what this movie would have done to the already tainted image of motorcyclists had it received widespread distribution.

For all its potential to alarm, Anger's film proved to be moot. While Hollywood wasn't looking, the motorcycle industry was busy changing its image. The early 1960s Honda ad campaign, boasting "You Meet The Nicest People on a Honda," inundated the public with images of clean-cut youngsters enjoying motorcycling as a healthy outdoor sport no different than volleyball or swimming. The campaign, which proved that one didn't have to wear black leather or break the law to ride a two-wheeler, did much to foster sales of the smaller imported bikes, while further distancing mainstream motorcyclists from the outlaw bikers who had been depicted on screen. With these affordable Japanese commuter bikes at the helm, the motorcycle industry entered one of its biggest and most sustained sales booms during the early 1960s. The increased, (and very inoffensive) presence of the new generation of motorcycles on America's Main Streets made it inevitable that bikes would show up in films with increasing regularity. Elvis Presley, one of the screen's biggest stars, led the way, carousing and romancing a slew of beauties aboard one of Honda's ubiquitous 350 Superhawks in *Roustabout* (1964). And

reactionary hypocrites who warn their daughters about mixing with their low-life biker neighbors while secretly envying the bikers freewheeling lifestyle. But it's not the neighborhood's nubile daughters the bikers are after, but the total domination of planet Earth (as is the goal of all extraterrestrials, which this bike gang proves to be). Determined to contaminate the world's fresh water supply and hold human beings for ransom, these bikers make Brando's Black Rebels seem like Tupperware salesmen.

Another film that is often ignored in discussions of early biker movies was filmmaker-author Kenneth Anger's abstract short *Scorpio Rising* (1962). If released today, it could have entered heavy rotation on MTV as an extended, fifteen-minute music video. Instead, Anger's homoerotic while it was not a biker movie per se, Steve McQueen's WWII prison wall jump (made by Bud Ekins) on an old Triumph twin in *The Great Escape* (1963) was one of cycling's great screen moments.

This grace period where motorcycles could be used in films for innocuous effect would prove to be short-lived, however. With beatniks, civil rights and an escalating war in Vietnam to contend with, the leather-jacketed biker gang of the 1950s was growing stale as fodder for the big screen. There would have to be some big, newsworthy fissures in the biker world for Hollywood to come calling again.

And filmmakers would get them, sooner than anticipated.

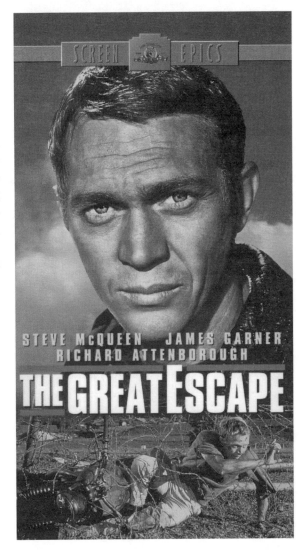

"With your cooperation we may all sit out the war very comfortably."
German Commandant to his prisoners
The Great Escape

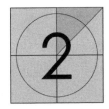

Hide Your Daughters!

The Psychedelic Sixties and Seventies

Whether movies follow trends or create them is one of pop culture's great chicken-egg arguments. The debate over the role of anti-social movies in creating an anti-social populace has emerged periodically ever since Paul Muni frightened authorities and dazzled Depression-era moviegoers with his riveting portrayal of an amoral gangster in *Scarface* (1932). Parent's groups tend to rationalize that if you cut off access to the irresponsible, violent films that youths emulate, delinquency will disappear overnight.

This message fell on deaf ears at the oft-struggling Hollywood offices of American International Pictures. The maverick film studio was a study in ambivalence and artistic contradiction: since forming in the early 1950s, Jim Nicholson (no relation to actor Jack) and a former attorney and movie buff Samuel Z. Arkoff had foisted on the world a catalog of the world's worst horror films, including *I Was a Teenage Werewolf* (1957), and the world's most popular teen comedies, with its Frankie Avalon-Annette Funicello *Beach Party* series. Nicholson and Arkoff knew all too well what role movies played in the public psyche and they weren't about to let national fears of *youth gone wild* stop them from mining the headlines for script fodder.

In fact, as studio heads went, the boisterous, cigar-chomping Arkoff wasn't bound to the usual

pretensions affecting movie moguls who struggled to placate powerful investors and newspaper columnists by releasing only morally upright films. Instead, American International made no secret of making movies assembly-line style, releasing pulp with titles like *The Brain that Wouldn't Die* (1963). At a time when censors routinely re-titled films deemed too suggestive, A.I.P. churned out *The Naked Invader* (1958) and advertised the film with openly provocative lobby cards and posters.

The studio knew that the teen exploitation and juvenile delinquent films of the 1950s were scandalous enough in that straightlaced, Eisenhower era, but by the early 1960s, they had been rendered little more than quaint period pieces when compared to reality. The Beat Generation, with its condemnation of middle-class values, open embrace of sex and drugs, and its wild, otherworldly aesthetic, was transforming a nation's youth into something alien and foreign to most Americans. Arkoff and Nicholson wagered that people would line up for blocks to see just how strange the kids had become.

At the forefront of the new generation's quirks and passions were the motorcycle gangs, a new breed of delinquent whose anti-social exploits were appearing in the very newspapers delivered to Nicholson's and Arkoff's studios.

Director Roger Corman, (left) and Peter Bogdanovich (right) instruct Peter Fonda on the finer points of chopper riding in 1966's *The Wild Angels.* **The film and a subsequent drug bust proved a major image makeover for the squeaky-clean Fonda. (American International Pictures)**

The filmmakers were learning that the leather-jacketed hoodlums of *The Wild One* hadn't ceased to exist, but in the decade or so since Brando immortalized the outlaw biker on film, a cultural change had also occurred amongst two wheelers. The change, which affected everything from the types of motorcycles bikers rode to the way they treated the public and each other was so significant, it's unlikely Brando's Black Rebels would have recognized much of themselves in Peter Fonda's *Wild Angels.*

Just like Stanley Kramer after the Hollister Riot, a young director named Roger Corman realized the real-life exploits of the new motorcycle subculture might have the pulling power to fill a few theater seats. Corman, having directed several B-grade horror movies and westerns throughout the early 1950s for American International Pictures, had just signed on with big-hitters Columbia Pictures who were looking for a director to make formula Westerns. However, Corman saw a screenplay just waiting to be plucked from the real lives of the Hell's Angels. Corman was known as an open-minded young director who could bring even an under-funded film in under budget. His work on the Western *Apache Woman* (1955) and schlock horror classics like *Attack of the Crab Monsters* (1957) had been keeping A.I.P. afloat, but Corman was ready to try something more timely.

With novelist Hunter S. Thompson's biographical *Hell's Angels* shooting up the best-seller charts in the summer of 1966, Corman saw a definitive biker photo in an issue of *Life* magazine. The image of a solemn, menacing column of choppers rolling into a California cemetery for the funeral of a dead biker was enough to spur Corman and writer Charles Griffith to create an entire screenplay, Corman has said. A deal was made between the two studios so Corman could be released from his duties at Columbia long enough to shoot the biker movie for American International—and the first real outlaw motorcycle film was on its way. The appearance of hairy-chested, beer-fueled biker hordes in pop culture couldn't have occurred at a better time. Studio heads at A.I.P. knew that Westerns and sci-fis were quickly playing themselves out. Instead, the studio hit upon a formula where "we started looking for our audience by removing the element of authority in our films. We saw the rebellion coming, but we couldn't predict the extent of it so we made a rule: no parents, no church, or authorities in our films," said Arkoff. Instead, the A.I.P. team targeted reckless and would-be reckless youths with a roster of movies where anyone old, professional, or representing The Man was an ineffectual buffoon with no clue whatsoever what real kicks were. It was this "Lord of the Flies" approach to storytelling that Corman and Arkoff utilized for their first foray into the biker movie genre, *The Wild Angels* (1966).

Timing also proved to be on American International's side as the Hell's Angels continued to show up in newspapers while the film was in the planning stages. A well-publicized rape of two teenage girls during a 1964 Labor Day Hell's Angels rally at Monterey, California caused the California Attorney General's office to report on the outlaw biker gangs, and cement the club's reputation with the public as a bunch of hard-drinking miscreants. This explains the gratuitous sexual innuendoes in *The Wild Angels*. One couldn't blame Corman for playing on the fears surrounding the rape case to help sell his film to people who were no doubt familiar with the trial. Corman's gamble worked, and in time, the omnivorous sexual appetites of outlaw bikers—real or imagined—would become a common stereotype, with nearly every biker movie following *The Wild Angels* containing a rape, orgy, or scene involving a biker sharing his ol' lady.

While the public's disapproving view of—and curiosity about—outlaw bikers almost guaranteed an audience for the film, Corman's way was made that much clearer by the outlandish look of

the real bikers themselves. Casting and costumes couldn't have invented more camera-ready villains: Nazi insignias, dirty denims, and plenty of scowling, unshaven faces were enough to cause every teenager in America to rush to the nearest box office, cash in hand.

Of course, before *The Wild Angels* could begin production, the filmmakers had to conduct a little field research. Approaching members of outlaw bike clubs, Corman said, was one of the toughest casting calls in all of moviedom. This was long before the days of media-hungry, self-reverential outlaw bikers who routinely appear on talk shows and as consultants to films. So Corman took a lead from Hunter Thompson and offered a group of bikers a sidecar full of cold beer to open up about their lives. Corman described the ensuing interviews as illuminating, having seldom encountered so many crazy, spontaneous characters before.

> "To be free, to ride our machines without being hassled by the man. And, to get loaded."
> Heavenly Blues (Peter Fonda)
> *The Wild Angels*

Shooting the initial outlaw biker film was an unproven enterprise, an undertaking so filled with potential (and as time would prove, actual) mishaps, the making of *The Wild Angels* would have probably made a better film than the feature itself. When production began in Mecca, California, Nicholson and Corman had decided to offer several members of the Venice chapter of the Hell's Angels parts as extras. However, the two intellectual filmmakers were well aware of the predatory tendencies of bike gangs, so they made a secret deal with two beefy club enforcers to keep errant members in line. They were also savvy enough to change the film's proposed name from "Angry Angels" to avoid making restitution payments to the club.

But before the first camera rolled, production was nearly shut down by local sheriff's deputies who showed up on the set with arrest warrants for several of the bikers working on the film. The cops were persuaded to let the bikers work, but soon thereafter, the famous father of co-star Nancy Sinatra showed up on the set with two of his own stout bodyguards in tow. Sinatra, never a

As biker films go, *Wild Angels* is something of a breakthrough even though it bears much of the stilted acting and exaggerated action of many a Corman classic. Part of this can be attributed to his lead, Peter Fonda. The famous second-generation actor was known as a decidedly square young bloke who was looking to change his image after starring in several squeaky-clean teen romance flicks. Corman chose Fonda for the part of Heavenly Blues (named, oddly, after a variety of Morning Glory seed) only after learning that the film's first choice, *West Side Story* star George Chikaris could not ride a motorcycle. Looking very dated in a longish Beatle haircut, Fonda manages to pull off being the brooding, outlaw gang leader with his cool, understated approach to acting. Fonda was aided by Corman's dedication to presenting an objective view of the bikers; the entire script, even after an extensive re-write by Peter Bogdanovich, contained only 120 lines of dialogue.

What *The Wild Angels* did contain in large doses were shots of the club "playing biker;" open kissing between male members, constant threats and challenges to the "citizens," and plenty of spirited riding. The greasy clothes, bawdy come-ons and unconventional living arrangements of "Loser" (Bruce Dern) and his old lady Gaysh, (played by real-life wife Diane Ladd), who share their grubby sofa and floor with any of the brothers who happen by, were enough to shock middle America as few films had. The film follows a simple story line that's so indistinct, a narrative is hard to establish. Dern's Loser is on the trail of his stolen chopper which he and Fonda learn has been swiped by a group of Mexicans. The pair find the stolen Hog, but during the fight to recover it, the cops happen by and a chase ensues. Loser steals a police motorcycle and is seriously wounded by a patrolman's bullet during a well-paced chase in the foothills above Hollywood.

The gang decides to bust Loser out of the hospital, and in classic style, they pause to molest a nurse who's unfortunate enough to be assigned to the biker ward that night. But after Loser is returned to the gang's hangout, he dies from lack of hospital care, and from the constant partying that the bikers seem committed to. The rest of *The Wild*

fan of 1960s youth culture, had attempted to talk Nancy out of appearing in *The Wild Angels*. When this didn't work, Sinatra's visit made it very clear to Corman that if any of the motorcycle hoodlums touched his daughter, there would be dire consequences. In a 1999 interview on cable television's Discovery Channel, Corman related an incident where his sometimes curt orders were less than well-received by the biker-actors. With feelings on the set in a constant state of tension, the bikers decided to throw a few real punches at a hapless assistant script writer, Peter Bogdanovich, during the movie's final fight scene.

Once the multitude of obstacles were out of the way, Corman was determined to create a film that neither condemned nor glorified the biker gangs—audiences were to draw their own conclusions from the images presented on the screen.

Angels is one long funeral march, with the surviving club members struggling to lug their compatriot's corpse back to the small northern California town of his birth. The townsfolk, being conservative squares and all, would rather host a Nation of Islam convention than entertain a biker gang funeral, establishing the constant threat that the bikers will be run out of town before they can bury Loser in true club style.

The movie culminates in a daring sequence filmed in a church where a priest is coerced, under threat of a good stomping, to perform last rites on the quickly rotting biker. Just before the bikers destroy the church in an orgy of spilled beer, drugs, busted pews, and before Loser's old lady is gang-raped in the church, Fonda delivers a timeless, outlaw biker manifesto about "wanting to be free from the hassles of The Man." That single monologue has become so revered among counterculturalists it's been sampled by numerous rock and alternative bands and included on dozens of albums over the years. At the film's end, the gang brawls with a crew of angry townspeople who've emerged to take their church back before the bikers hop on their choppers to evade the police. Blues, along with Mike, are the only two who don't run. The pair can't seem to muster the energy to run away from responsibility any longer. The final scene was the source of much speculation by highbrow critics as it showed the bikers realizing their nihilism was a dead-end street. Worse yet, Corman and Bogdanovich were in danger of being taken seriously as filmmakers.

Shot in just over two weeks, (and, at times, looking that way) *Wild Angels* created a sensation nonetheless. When screened at the 1966 Venice Film Festival, the U.S. State Department attempted to dissuade Nicholson and Arkoff from showing the movie as it revealed a side of American life not exactly conducive with their notions of democracy and citizenship. While *Wild Angels* was panned by many critics—*Newsweek* discredited it as "an ugly piece of trash,"—the movie was easily as outrageous and popular with moviegoers as *The Wild One* had been little more than a decade earlier. At drive-ins and theaters throughout the state of California where the motorcycle gangs were most prevalent, the movie was proving so popular Arkoff had to turn away some requests for copies which the surprised studio couldn't print fast enough.

And just as things were heating up at the box office, Peter Fonda was arrested and charged with possession of marijuana. Fonda's bust helped build more interest in the drug-culture film, which was the lucky recipient of dual publicity from both legal reporters and writers on the entertainment page. Hip outlaw bikers at the time, of course, were already consumed by the lifestyle Corman had brought to national prominence and saw the usual parody and oversimplification of their lives as half-funny and half-exploitative. The real-life Hell's Angels, however, found very little to laugh about, especially after the record-setting box office receipts (the film grossed $5 million in its opening month before becoming one of A.I.P.'s highest grossing films ever) started rolling in.

After ending their relationship with Thompson on a sour note and failing to collect the three kegs of beer he had promised in return for access to their private lives, the Hell's Angels were not about to have their name, reputations, and images capitalized upon without getting their fair share. Members of the San Bernardino chapter immediately filed a lawsuit seeking $2 million in compensation from A.I.P. The bikers claimed, incredibly, that their character had been irreparably defamed by the film's portrayal of motorcycle gangs. It was a tough call for lawyers on both sides, since Corman's dramatizations of outlaw biker life were part real, and partly drawn from the exaggerations in the press. The director himself said that the bikers he interviewed before filming were so pleased at the chance to impress a "straight" filmmaker that they ended up embellishing most of their personal stories either out of habit or self-aggrandizement. But even if Corman was simply following his pre-production consultations with the bikers, the Hell's Angels proved to be, like most, people who didn't care to see themselves portrayed on film as anything but heroes.

In the past, outlaw bikers settled these sorts of differences with their steel-toed boots instead of through high-powered attorneys, but now the Hell's Angels let word spread throughout L.A. that Corman and Arkoff where marked for death

Is the female of the species deadlier than the male? seemed to ask 1969's *Hell's Belles.* **Starring Jeremy Slate, the film was a barely-disguised remake of the 1950 Jimmy Stewart western** *Winchester '73.* **(Orion Pictures)**

unless a tribute was paid to them for providing impetus for *The Wild Angels.* Corman, for his part, continued to play the clever raconteur, deflecting the death threats by explaining to the angry bikers that if he was dead, it was unlikely they'd ever collect the money they felt he owed them. Corman's argument proved so persuasive, members of several chapters accepted a $2,000 out-of-court settlement. They also proved unable to resist publicity with president Ralph "Sonny" Barger readily signing on to work on several of A.I.P.'s successive outlaw motorcycle gang features.

> "Recognize those bikes? No. They're like men—they're all the same."
> Lady bikers
> *Hell's Belles*

Following the timeworn Hollywood axiom, "if it works, beat it to death," American International Pictures quickly set to work on *The Devil's Angels* (1967). Maverick young director John Cassavetes was lined up for the lead role and began shooting while *The Wild Angels* was still in theaters. Once the money started rolling in, the studio attacked the biker movie genre with the same verve and assembly-line approach it had the monster movie and the Western a decade before. In all, Arkoff and Nicholson were to release over a dozen biker movies to varying levels of box-office success before the genre played itself out in the mid 1970s.

In a strange coincidence, the Westerns that biker movies were intended to replace would forever shadow the biker movie genre, with Arkoff's now-solvent studio simply re-routing many of the producers, directors, crew and even actors from its horse operas onto choppers for the new generation of action-adventure films. A.I.P. was adept at moving its workers around like a basketball coach improvising a new defense; screenwriter James Gordon White, who would pen the script for *Hell's Belles* (1969) borrowed the narrative from the Western *Winchester '73* (1950) while longtime A.I.P. Western actor Jock Mahoney was pulled out of the stagecoach to star in the biker movie *The Glory Stompers*. And critics had a field day exposing the similarities between the 1968 biker flick *Chrome and Hot Leather* and *The Magnificent Seven* (1960). The two genres even played to similar audiences with American International Pictures' film distributors racking up the highest box-office figures from theaters throughout the American Midwest and in the Deep South. These were the same areas where films like *Gunslinger* (1956) had done well. Audiences in the East and those in big cities never played much of a role in the emergence of the biker movie.

For riders on the road at the time, the movies had a profound effect, both on the way they perceived themselves and on the public's view of bikers. The radically customized chopper, for instance, was already at the core of a cottage industry in California where the majority of the biker movies were being produced. Though odd paint jobs and lengthy modifications to individual motorcycles were nothing new to motorcycling, the West Coast chopper look, which emphasized flash over comfort, was first seen by millions of bikers at the local movie house. Bikes as fully altered as Fonda's Harley-Davidson Panhead chopper in *The Wild Angels* which were long on forks and short on suspension and braking systems, were still a regional phenomenon, as custom motorcycle magazines like *Easyriders* and aftermarket parts suppliers were still nearly a decade away. Arlen Ness, perhaps California's best-known motorcycle customizer, was just getting started with his chopper fabricating business at the time *The Wild Angels* was released. Ness, now an international phenomenon with his machines featured in museums and selling for upward of six figures, said the machines in the early biker movies were usually built by small, backyard custom wizards like himself. Others were owned by the real-life bikers who worked as security guards and extras in the films.

And as the movies exposed to the world what a few mechanical geniuses in California could do to a stock Harley or Britbike, Ness said, "Most people had never seen a chopper before, but after these Peter Fonda movies, there was hardly a motorcycle on the streets that didn't have a front brake removed or a sissy bar three-feet tall. It was wild. Every time a new movie came out, the guys would go to see it to kind of keep up with the Joneses to see what the other guys were building." In a few years, Ness and dozens of others were taking the custom, crushed velvet seats,

HE'S OUT TO FIND THE GANG THAT RIPPED HIM OFF.

BUT YOU DON'T FIND THEM, THEY FIND YOU!

NEW! DIGITALLY REMASTERED VERSION

psychedelic paint jobs, raked and stretched frames, and narrow springer front forks that had captured imaginations in the movies to the masses with a burgeoning chopper parts business. That it took small, private garages several years to help spread the California chopper look across the country is evident of how self-consciously the movie industry now markets itself. It is difficult to imagine Hollywood churning out several dozen popular motorcycle genre films today without at least a fast food marketing tie-in and a limited-edition, stretch chopper to mimic the ones featured in films.

And it wasn't just the motorcycles that moviegoers emulated. In his 1982 biography *Fallen Angel*, Hell's Angel-turned-televangelist Barry Mayson described being a bored automotive plant laborer in Georgia before catching *Hell's*

"Tough to resist!" - Leonard Maltin

Angels on Wheels at a local drive-in. Mayson, who had never before ridden a motorcycle, promptly picked up a second-hand BSA 650 and set out to become "just like a modern-day outlaw." "These guys were anything but hippies," he wrote of his first introduction to movie bikers. "They were pirates, with the highways for the high seas, taking what they wanted and going where they pleased." Mayson's obsession with the way the screen outlaws looked and lived struck him—and countless thousands of others—such that he spent much of the next decade attempting to recreate their exploits in his own life. Mayson concedes that long hair and earrings weren't exactly acceptable in 1968 Georgia, but the need to fashion his image as unabashedly macho like that of the movie biker was enough to make Mayson discard societal norms. As American International Pictures cranked out *The Devil's Angels* in 1967, motorcycle gangs resembling the movie bikers were starting to become visible in cities all across America. Of course, many had been in existence for decades before Peter Fonda donned an Iron Cross and a smirk. New York's Queensboro Motorcycle Club, for example, could trace its origins back to the 1920s board track racing scene, while hundreds of other AMA-affiliated motorcycle clubs had little but disdain for the whole chopper movement and the movies that glorified it.

But the fashions and stylings of the outlaw clubs based on the films seemed to grow exponentially during this period, with chrome Nazi helmets, scraggly beards, and the ubiquitous, sleeveless denim vest appearing almost everywhere at once. In *Buttons: The Making of a President*, Jamie Mandelkau wrote that the Hell's Angels movies provided British bikers with their first glimpse of American-style motorcycle outlaws. His autobiographical tale of the emerging UK outlaw scene chronicles his transition from a Rocker to a man so inspired by what he'd seen at the local cinema, he started the UK's first official Hell's Angels chapter.

As the biker movies spread to worldwide audiences, Mandelkau was soon joined by imitation outlaw gangs, fashioned after American movie bikers and making themselves known in Australia and throughout Europe. Many gangs have persevered, eventually establishing links with

As real outlaw motorcycle gangs made headlines across America, American International Pictures rushed several biker exploitation movies into production. Following the success of *The Wild Angels* (1966) came John Cassavetes in *The Devil's Angels* (1967). (American International Pictures)

their U.S. forebearers. With biker movies making a moderately strong showing at the box office and audiences crying for more, the follow up to *The Wild Angels* would be little more than a sequel, varying little from the original. *Devil's Angels* (1967) shared not only the bikers-invade-a-small, hick-town theme of *The Wild Angels,* but it also had a screenplay written by *Wild Angels* author Charles Griffith, and an instrumental rock-guitar soundtrack by Davie Allen and the Arrows.

Director Daniel Haller further sets the biker movie template by utilizing a relatively spare script and a storyline which seems intended only to set up the various biker lifestyle scenes audiences craved. *The Devil's Angels* is rife with long, panoramic shots of the Skulls guzzling beers, whooping it up on their choppers, and inevitably ransacking the recreational vehicle of some hapless travelers. Again, the Hell's Angels' Monterey rape trial was mined for impact as the Skulls, who

enjoy the company of a few adventuresome teenage girls from the small town, are accused of raping one of them. The gang, after being run off by the town's cops and attacked by local rednecks, is aided by another biker gang to set up a "court" where the girl is forced to admit she lied about the alleged rape. But before they let her go and head out of town, one of the bikers rationalizes that being acquitted of a false rape is not as much fun as the real thing so he decides, "We got us a rape coming!"

Just like Fonda at the conclusion of *The Wild Angels* Cassavetes decides he's had enough of the mindless brutishness of his club brothers and opts out of the melee just moments before police sirens approach in the distance. Like A.I.P.'s previous release, *The Devil's Angels* explores the darker side of the rootless, vagrant outlaw lifestyle. Cassavetes' Cody pauses several times to lament how many members of the club have been "arrested or croaked." The constant reminder by authorities to "just move along down the road" had been made painfully real when *Rolling Stone* magazine ran a full-page photo of the Monterey, California Hell's Angels being escorted out of town by sheriff's deputies. It's worth noting that Haller's movie was also a more visually arresting sight than *The Wild Angels* with most of the footage being shot in the bright, winter sunshine of the California desert.

Cassavetes plays Cody with a permanently furrowed brow and the learned, clean-shaven intelligence that would characterize many biker movie gang leaders. It was as if directors needed to separate the gang leaders from the unwashed rank and file by imbuing the characters with an almost aloof ability to see through the whole charade, and, if need be, opt back into a better life when things got too hot.

Following close on the rear fender of *The Devil's Angels* was *Hell's Angels on Wheels* (1967), which was the first major-release biker movie that didn't arrive bearing the expected American International logo. What this US Films feature did bring to the table was Jack Nicholson, a talented young writer-actor whose portrayal of the sensitive biker Poet is one of the genre's (few) outstanding performances. Producer Joe Solomon broke ranks with Corman and other filmmakers who avoided using the real outlaw gang's name as part of their movie's titles. Soloman actually one-upped Corman's use of the Angels as script advisors and on-set extras by paying the club several thousand dollars for the use of its name and hiring the entire Oakland, California chapter to appear in a goofy opening sequence.

The credits pause to acknowledge club president Sonny Barger as "technical advisor" as he dramatically dismounts his chopper to embrace actor Adam Rourke. From there, things definitely move on an upward trajectory as *Hell's Angels on Wheels* displays a rare commodity in early biker movies: a plot! *Hell's Angels On Wheels* centers on a week or so in the life of Nicholson's Poet, a

> "I think a lot of you."
> "Well don't."
> Poet (Jack Nicholson) and
> Shill (Sabrina Scharf)
> *Hell's Angels on Wheels*

deep-thinking gas station attendant whose boss fires him for getting too lippy with a customer, a scene which transpires while a group of Angels ransack the store. Adam Rourke is Buddy, performing a John Cassavetes impersonation he would reprise several times in biker movies. As the gang's president, Buddy invites Poet to join the Angels on the road as a club hangaround, an offer the Harley-riding loner accepts with casual indifference.

Poet seems to have it all: he can handle himself in a brawl, he has a pretty cool bike and even a nickname ready-made for initiation into the outlaw brotherhood. But, like Hollywood's proverbial whore with the heart of gold, Poet has a weak spot for a damsel in distress. In this instance, the distressed damsel is Sabrina Scharf, who is alternately alluring and infuriating as Shill, Rourke's notoriously fickle ol' lady who looks more like a Vassar humanities major than an outlaw's moll.

Poet is so chivalrous he declines to make it with Shill because her spaced-out roommate is watching. "I think a lot of you," he confesses during an embrace. "Well don't," she shoots back, with all the nonchalance of a female version of Brando's Johnny.

Nicholson's portrayal of the gentleman outlaw is a character that filmmakers would return to for inspiration some 20 years later when outlaw biker movies would adopt a more sympathetic view of their protagonists (see chapter 6). True to form, Poet won't let Shill's lack of morals derail his quest for love. He's driven to rescue her from the gang, while Shill is driven to rescue Buddy, who "only wants people to do as I tell them." With Buddy's self-reverential egotism and a script that has the Angels getting involved in more impromptu brawls than a Spinks family reunion (five punch-outs occur within the first quarter of the film with the Angels, naturally, winning each one) there's little wonder this was the first biker movie the club actually endorsed. Barger himself embarked on a one-man public relations crusade to convince other bikers to see *Hell's Angels on Wheels*. What effect this had on the film's moderately successful box-office run is anyone's guess. *Hell's Angels on Wheels*, with its breezy, flute-jazz soundtrack by the Stu Phillips Orchestra and long, playful scenes of the bikers rolling through lush green countryside, further solidifies the patterns most of the biker films would follow. There's the misguided gang, basically just looking for understanding, there's the demanding, intelligent leader, and the eternal conflict with the damsel in distress. *Hell's Angels on Wheels* also includes stock biker movie conventions such as the biker wedding, complete with a Harley-Davidson parts manual replacing the bible and the first screen appearance of Jack Starrett as the solemn, drawling Lt. Bingham. Starrett, who made a career in motorcycle gang movies showing up apparently just to make wise cracks, would replay this role in a half-dozen biker movies, eventually resurrecting the same mean-spirited character as Officer Gualt in Sylvester Stallone's *First Blood* in 1982.

Where Director Richard Rush broke convention was with his staid reliance on pop-culture film techniques of the day. During one of the movie's countless brawls, the Angels tangle with the Madcaps gang to a whimsical soundtrack, mixing moments of slapstick, uneven camera angles, and fast-motion shooting with violence. The end effect is similar to the campy, well-choreographed fight scenes from the old *Batman* series starring Adam West. And for sheer laughs, Rush's attempts to capture the carefree spirit of the Flower Child generation are unparalleled. During one club run, Shill is so overwhelmed by the beauty of the California countryside that she leaps from a chopper to hug a sheep grazing by the highway. "Oh you beautiful sheep!" she exclaims, a line the actress likely regretted uttering for the remainder of her brief career. In the end, poor, kindhearted Poet learns that Shill's loyalties cannot be swayed from the club, despite how badly she's often treated. In a closing fight scene, she offers assistance to Buddy instead of Poet, perhaps to remind audiences that outlaws will always stick with their own kind. The film did more for the career of Jack Nicholson than the Hell's Angels. By the fall of 1967, he was actually on the set of another biker movie, this time, taking a supporting role in the less well-known *Rebel Rousers*.

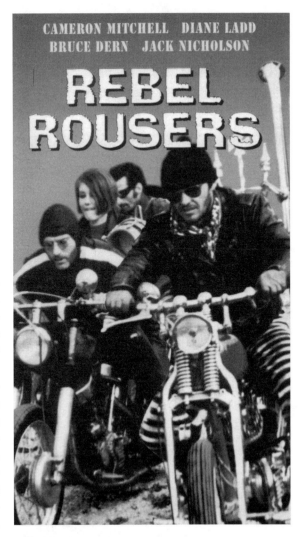

The film didn't reach theaters until 1970, at which point the artistic and commercial success of *Easy Rider* had relegated these early biker movies to a lesser status.

Rebel Rousers, compared to Nicholson's other work in biker movies, is a dismal little time-waster that easily reveals why it didn't generate the sort of interest of his other two biker movie roles. Set in the desert hamlet of Chloride, California, *Rebel Rousers* plays its hand fairly early, with Bruce Dern as a repentant gang leader, and Nicholson sort of fading into the background as Bunny, a blood-thirsty gang member. It seems the half-dozen Rebel Rousers are, like most movie bikers, determined to make trouble in some faraway little hick town. They arrive in the sparsely populated burg at approximately the same time as Dern's (J.J.) old high school football buddy

Paul Collier (played by film baddie Cameron Mitchell). Collier is in Chloride to reconcile with his pregnant, hard-drinking wife Karen, played by a weepy Diane Ladd. If the bikers in both of Nicholson's first two movies were faithfully accurate recreations of the real thing, Martin Cohen, director of the *Rebel Rousers* seems to have had little familiarity with actual outlaws. The gang consists of a contemplative Jew (called, appropriately, The Hebrew) who rides around wearing a jacket from a concentration camp prisoner's uniform, a mock cowboy, Dern in the same greasy white sweatshirt he wore in *The Wild Angels*, Nicholson wearing black-and-white striped prisoner's pants, and character actor Harry Dean Stanton, in an inspired turn as a gay biker dressed in a suit and tie! The gang inevitably runs into Paul and Bunny on the beach where the depraved bikers decide to have their way with the pregnant woman (another factoid borrowed from the Hell's Angels' Monterey rape trial where one of the alleged victims was seven months pregnant). Dern's quiet rebel, however, spends the tiresome remainder of the movie trying to stall his bros from their intended act of degeneracy.

It didn't really matter what *Rebel Rousers* did or did not have to say. By then the template had been set and the studios were determined to crank out as long a list of biker movies as audiences would continue to pay for. Some were better and some easily worse than *Rebel Rousers*, but the genre was just starting to roll. In the next few years, the movies came as fast and relentlessly as the studios could find financing for them.

It wasn't hard to find backers considering the grosses biker films were generating, the biggest of which proved to be A.I.P.'s *Born Losers* (1967), which was the first of writer-director-actor Tom Laughlin's white knight roles as the half-breed Indian activist Billy Jack. In *Born Losers*, which dragged former seductress Jane Russell out of semi-retirement and girdle advertisements, Laughlin is the lone hero who's man enough to stand up against a biker gang led by Jeremy Slate. Slate's gang is so foul, they have members with names like Gangrene and Crabs—that, and a penchant for gang rape. Laughlin does a respectable-if-dullish turn as the solemn hero, arriving too late to save airline stewardess-turned-actress

Elizabeth James from the bikers. The rape-rescuer scenario was more than just a fantasy for Laughlin; he borrowed impetus for the story from a real-life incident where a former marine from Philadelphia took up arms against an outlaw biker gang who were terrorizing local women. The role was perfect for Laughlin, who history remembers as a maverick filmmaker unable to discern where Billy Jack ended and his creator began. The former bit-part regular eventually used his sanctimonious, left-leaning revenge fantasies to capture the imagination of millions with his self-titled 1970s release *Billy Jack.* The second film did so well under Laughlin's orchestrated release that *Born Losers* received an encore run alongside the sequel. *Born Losers*, however, was Laughlin's sole use of bikers. By the time *Billy Jack* hit the screen, he'd moved on to protecting communes full of hippies and Native Americans from a town's redneck sheriff.

American International Pictures, by now the recognized granddaddy of the biker movie, continued to exploit its leadership status by offering audiences *Mini Skirt Mob* (1968), which pits Jeremy Slate against Sherry Jackson's vicious, all-female motorcycle gang, and *The Glory Stompers* (1968) which featured Dennis Hopper's first biker movie role as the maniacal leader of the Black Souls Motorcycle Club. Hopper, in an obvious nod to Lee Marvin's *Wild One* character, is named Chino and plays like a version of that character with his nose buried in a methamphetamine jar. Hopper's gang is responsible for kidnapping the girlfriend of Daryl, the Stompers president (Jody McRea). The ensuing chase leads the Stompers to a dusty field in Mexico where the girlfriend in question has been sold into slavery. A fight ensues at a communal bathing hole the club uses, giving birth to one of the only scenes in all biker moviedom that combines nudity, violence, *and* motorcycle crashes.

The Glory Stompers has little to remember except for introducing film producer and later, legendary Top 40 deejay Casey Kasem to audiences as Mouth, a fast-talking member of the Black Souls. Hearing Kasem deliver his menacing lines in the same voice that would later detail the rise of Duran Duran and Michael Jackson up the pop music charts is one of the weirder moments in

Biker movie regulars Jeremy Slate (second from left) and Robert Tessier (center) appear alongside self-styled screen hero Billy Jack (Tom Laughlin) in 1967's *Born Losers*. **(American International Pictures)**

biker movies. Even weirder moments were to come, however. Barely concealed remakes of remakes flooded the screen with tasteless, poorly-acted films like Russ Meyer's *Motor Psycho* (1968) starring West Side Story lead Russ Tamblyn, and *The Cycle Savages* (1969) which again saw Bruce Dern as a drug-crazed gang leader, this time abducting teenage beauties whom he promptly sells into white slavery. Often, American International Pictures changed little between filmings, with actors and actresses sporting the same haircuts, or even riding the same motorcycles that were used in a production just weeks—or in some instances, days—before.

Some variations in the town invasion theme did occur, and occasionally directors imbued their biker movies with contemporary social issues. This was the case with the Dick Clark (yes, that Dick Clark) production *The Savage Seven*.

Here, Adam Rourke reprises his cool, cocky gang leader role from *Hell's Angels on Wheels*, but this time his girlfriend is a Native American woman (Joanna Frank) who causes outbreaks of prejudice, not passion, amongst everyone she meets, including some of the club's own mammas. For a change, the bikers fight the good fight, defending her honor and that of several Indian townspeople against yet another group of irrational, brawling rednecks. And when the gang is approached by Mr. Filmore—a crooked, sweaty town boss—to run the Indians off their oil-rich ancestral lands, the gang decides to act. After spending an afternoon partying and sharing some tribal tests of machismo with the local tribe, the bikers end up realizing that, as outcasts, they've got a lot more in common with the Indians than they do the rednecks. The two groups forge a hokey, and very New Age, "spiritual bond" with the Indians, a

Tom Stern as Mike (left) and Ted Markland (right) as Smiley lead their rag-tag gang the Madcaps on an ill-fated quest to take over all the world's motorcycle gangs in *Angels From Hell*, a 1968 release. (American International Pictures)

link that many real bikers, for some reason, believe exists to this day.

Unfortunately, *The Savage Seven* relies almost entirely on fight scenes to supply action and flow, and too many of these identical head-smashing, knuckle-busting sequences leave viewers crying out for a few road shots. Penny Marshall, daughter of TV producer Garry, makes her screen debut in *Savage Seven* as a club mamma, but is left out as the film culminates in a messy, 20-minute free-for-all that has bikers, Indians, and rednecks wasting each other wholesale. In the end, Rourke's Kissum and Joanna Frank's Maria ride off into the moonlight, leaving

> "When it becomes a crime to ride a motorcycle, it'll be a sad day for us all."
> Sheriff (Jack Starrett)
> *Angels From Hell*

hundreds of bruised and bloody combatants to heal their own—and society's—wounds.

Although most every movie during this period focused simply on exhausting proven formulas of town-invading bikers and the inevitable showdown with The Man, *Angels From Hell* (1968), offers a more realistic view of what many biker gangs were going through at the time. The story centers around returning Vietnam vet Tom Stern, who, after rescuing a gang of black bikers from the patrons of a redneck tavern, hooks up with his pre-war gang. Problem is, while Stern was away protecting democracy in the jungles of Southeast Asia, his

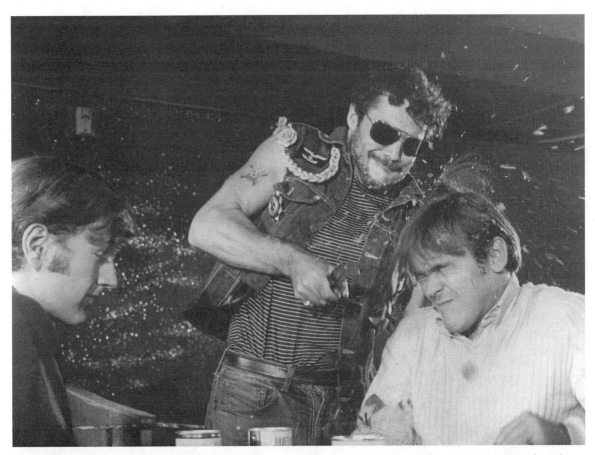

Borrowing plots, actors and even production crews from western films, most biker movies of the 1960s incorporated another time-honored western tradition—the barroom brawl. (*The Wild Rebels* **courtesy of Crown International Pictures**)

gang, like most outlaw clubs, was run out of town by the cops. In their new location, the Madcaps have developed a rather cozy relationship with the local constabulary, one they don't really care to alter. Stern, his eyes still filled with bloodlust, has megalomaniacal visions of forming a worldwide biker gang brotherhood, a force so strong it could topple the establishments and police departments from California to Ho Chi Min City.

While biker gangs reaching a state of relative peace with police departments was a tactic many adopted as mutually beneficial, the idea of establishing a single, worldwide outlaw gang was actually proposed by the Hell's Angels in the early 1990s, according to Canadian crime writer Yves Lavigne. In his often sensational book, *Hell's Angels At War*, Lavigne details the gang's ongoing efforts to consolidate hundreds of smaller outlaw gangs into the Angel fold. It was an ambitious

scheme, even for the world's largest biker gang, and one that *Angels from Hell* screenwriter Jerome Wish managed to foresee precisely some 25 years ahead of time.

In the movie version, Stern, as Mike, riding what looks like a Triumph Tiger prepped for off-road riding, slowly loses touch with reality when the club members shrug off his egotistical plan. But even as *Angels from Hell* degenerates into the usual montage of barroom brawls, violent chase scenes, and grungy biker schtick, director Bruce Kessler continues to add elements that move this film to a higher level. For instance, Mike's gang is invited to a poolside pot party at the home of a big shot Hollywood film producer who is interested in making a movie about cycle gangs. An obvious send-up of the interviews Roger Corman had conducted prior to the filming of *The Wild Angels*, it is one of the movies intentionally funnier

A clever look at the publicity onslaught facing outlaw bikers in the late 1960's was Fanfare Film's *Run Angel Run* where Angel, (William Smith) is hunted down by his gang after appearing in a magazine expose. (National Screen Service Corp)

moments. In *Angels from Hell,* American International Pictures reveals some of the tricks that the studio employed to save costs during the making of so many identical movies. The Madcaps' colors are the same worn by the gang who fought against Jack Nicholson and Adam Rourke in *Hell's Angels on Wheels,* while Stu Phillips again supplied a soundtrack of schmaltzy pop-jazz to a film that desperately cries out for some real rock and roll. Again, Jack Starrett is the deadpan sheriff who, in his meatiest part to date, utters another classic biker movie line, "When it becomes a crime to ride a motorcycle, it'll be a sad day for us all." There are also the obligatory shots filmed inside various go-go bars and clubhouse parties which, by now, offer few surprises. And the Madcaps, under Mike's tutelage, eventually disintegrate into a lion's den of in-fighting, domestic abuse, and enough screaming matches to fuel a season of *The Jenny Jones Show.*

Despite the many and obvious shortcomings, Ted Markland as Smiley (in a wicked pair of shades, one lens decorated with cross-hairs from a WWI machine-gun sight), and Stern manage to make a lot from a thin script and a budget lower than that of a high school production of *Cats.*

Many more films followed, with schlockmeister Herschel Gordon Lewis turning the macho creed of the bike gangs on its head with The Man-eaters, a group of nymphomaniac-sadists in *She Devils On Wheels* (1968). There was little to discern or distinguish films like *The Wild Rebels* (1967), *Angels Die Hard* (1970), or *Hell's Bloody Devils* (1970) with each borrowing from, and attempting to capitalize on, the success of other films.

One notable film from the deluge of biker movies in this period is *Run Angel, Run* (1969) a well-scripted release starring former bodybuilder-turned-actor William Smith. Smith plays Angel, a biker who sells out his gang to the tune of $10,000. Angel, president of the Devil's Advocates Motorcycle Club, gets his ugly mug pasted on the cover of *Like* magazine and earns cash for providing the lurid details for an investigative report on motorcycle gangs. This tongue-in-cheek thriller is not bad as a parody of a genre already taking itself too seriously, and Smith, with his gruff, Clint Eastwood-like delivery, gives one of his best performances.

Predictably, the gang doesn't care much for seeing their lifestyles recreated for the straights in a magazine (shades of the Hell's Angels' lawsuit against Corman after *Wild Angels*), so they decide to snuff the traitorous member before he does something really crazy like write a screenplay.

Run Angel, Run is a Fanfare Films production made by a crew of American International alumni, including movie cop Jack Starrett as director, Joe Solomon as producer, and Stu Phillips back at the bandstand as musical director. The result is actually a fairly engaging movie. First time director Starrett has all sorts of tricks up his sleeve for this 90-minute chase flick, splitting the screen into three, four and sometimes five separate viewing boxes for a timely psychedelic effect.

Country singer Tammy Wynette appears on the soundtrack during the art-imitating life segment where Smith, tired of running from and fighting with the gang, decides to take up a (relatively) quiet life restoring antique motorcycles in a small garage (much as real Hell's Angels President Ralph "Sonny" Barger would eventually do). Angel and his ol' lady (Valerie Starrett) find happiness in being a normal, working family, but the reverie is not to last: a final showdown with his old gang ruins his newfound, laxative-commercial lifestyle.

Always incorporating timely elements from the headlines, biker movies didn't ignore the escalating Vietnam conflict during the 1960s. The role of returning Vietnam vets in the biker gangs was first explored to mediocre effect in *Hell's Chosen Few* (1968) and to better lengths in a pair of A.I.P. releases that followed, *The Hard Ride* and

Chrome and Hot Leather, both from 1971. The former stars Robert Fuller as a faithful Vietnam infantry sergeant who returns home with the body of his black combat buddy in tow. Having been ensconced in the racially segregated world of outlaw biker gangs before the war, Fuller's solemn vet is determined to win his fallen buddy's place in society by having his white and Native American gang brothers attend the funeral. This is one of the few instances where heavy issues like civil rights and segregation found their way into a biker movie, and for all the propensity for preaching, director Burt Topper makes the most of his own lukewarm script.

Fuller's Phil is fortunate to inherit Lenny's "Baby," possibly the screen's most radical chopper ever, a bike so righteous one gang member remarks "I'd give up ballin' for a year for that

With headgear like this, there's little wonder why a team of Green Berets, including soul singer Marvin Gaye, waged war on biker gangs in *Chrome and Hot Leather*, a 1971 release. (American International Pictures)

mutha." And rightly so: Lenny's Harley-Davidson Knucklehead is about nine feet long with a swirling, metalflake paint job, a set of sky-high exhausts shaped like trombones and a front end so long it requires three head-lights and a four-lane boulevard to execute a turn. But handling the raked-out chopper is child's play compared to the rampant racism and thug-gery Fuller encounters around every turn. In be-tween his encounters with numerous Archie Bunker types, Fuller spends his days in some sce-nic cruises along northern California's highways and mountain passes. When his bike is pulled over by the state patrol, the kindly cop "only wanted to get a look at your bike" and the two end up chatting about chopper-building secrets.

"What's the matter with you—can't you see we're menacing someone?"
Chrome and Hot Leather

The scene is indicative of an overall call for unity in *The Hard Ride,* which made it a nice break from the mindless nihilism of the majority of biker movies. Fuller is determined to bury Lenny with his former club brothers in attendance, but it turns out they're all racists who care more about recovering Lenny's chopper than honoring a token black rider. Phil, as earnest as a Civil War abolitionist, ends up prevailing with his message of common decency, but only after several obligatory gang fights.

Chrome and Hot Leather is decidedly the lesser of the pair, with Tony Young as a Green Beret who takes on the motorcycle gang who murdered his fiancee. The Green Berets, just back from a tour in

parents of the same youth audiences they had initially targeted with their earlier biker movies.

The danger and iconoclasm the biker movie imbued on its actors when *The Wild Angels* was produced had softened so much that, by 1969, when *C.C. and Company* was produced, the National Football League encouraged its star quarterback, New York Jet Joe Namath, to appear in the film. Namath, who was one of professional sport's true modern superstars, was an all-American dude; his forays into New York clublife were legendary and his weekly TV talk show a ratings favorite. Even appearing opposite biker movie baddie William Smith couldn't tarnish Broadway Joe's heroic image. Namath, for his part, seldom does more in *C.C. and Company* to denigrate his name: he is shown shoplifting baked goods from a grocery store during a funny

'Nam, are blessed not only with martial skills that would shame James Bond, they've got the soulful voice of singer Marvin Gaye on their side. Even Gaye, however, can't save this one from a certain action flick corniness. These two films are worth mentioning because of their blatant portrayal of the military as heroic and cops as potentially decent people. Any filmmaker who wanted to stay on the cool side of the day's radical youth was taking one hell of a risk with scenes depicting cops and soldiers as anything but villains. These scenes might have reflected the advanced age of A.I.P.'s producers and directors, or maybe the political views of investors. Either way, it revealed that, by 1971, American International Pictures was quite possibly aiming their films at the

Tired of gang fights and chase scenes, (but apparently not loud sport shirts) American International Pictures' *The Hard Ride*, (1971) was groundbreaking in its call for racial and social unity. (American International Pictures)

opening sequence, but that's about it. By 1969 riding a chopper was considered not only cool but fashionable, and bedding his co-star, Vegas singer Ann-Margret couldn't have hurt Namath's playboy image much either.

Be the characterizations good or bad, real life biker outlaws were frequently perturbed with their portrayal on screen. The real Hell's Angels were given another chance to portray themselves on screen, but *Hell's Angels '69* (1969) changed little about their public face.

For all their legendary street antics, Barger and crew seem oddly intimidated by actually portraying themselves on screen. In scene after scene in this bank-heist caper, the Angels, with the possible exception of Terry The Tramp playing his psychotic self, managed to grind each episode to a painful, amateurish halt. *Hell's Angels '69* was the

brainchild of actor-writer Jeremy Slate who developed the script with the Angels in mind. Slate portrays Wes, and Tom Stern portrays Chuck as a pair of rich, idle bachelor brothers living a lifestyle straight out of *Playboy* magazine. Wes and Chuck tire of whizzing around in their Ferraris and dating beautiful women, so they decide to rob Caesar's Palace casino in Las Vegas for a break from their upperclass boredom. The pair concoct a fake motorcycle gang to provide cover—the Witches from Salem, Massachusetts—and hook up with the Angels for a few weeks of riding and scheming. Barger, acting with many of the club members featured in Thompson's book, generally *behave* rather than *act*, spending most of their energies guzzling beers and staging exaggerated embraces for the cameras.

Wes and Chuck never let the Angels in on the casino heist, which they pull off by assuming their true, clean-cut identities while the Angels fall easily as scapegoats. It's a clever idea that's unfortunately hamstrung by the aforementioned bad acting. Terry The Tramp, who seemed so menacing in Thompson's book, comes off as just plain goofy with his overanxious acting. Stern and Slate, with their beardless faces and spotless colors, are even less believable as bikers than the Angels are as actors.

While 1970s' *The Losers* doesn't star any actual Hell's Angels, the movie does draw its plot from an event that took place in the fall of 1966. After inveighing against a series of huge anti-War protest marches that occurred near their Oakland California headquarters, the Hell's Angels shocked their 60s counterculture contemporaries by offering their services to President Lyndon Johnson as "a special team of crack commandos." It's unknown what Johnson thought of the offer that Barger penned, but the hippies and flower children were shocked that their anti-establishment heroes turned out to be just as right wing as dear old dad. *The Losers*, filmed in the jungles of the Philippines, turns out to be nearly as bizarre as Barger's patriotic call to arms, with the four outlaws visiting Vietnam dressed in their typical gang garb. They soon set up a "clubhouse" in the jungle, complete with beer and cheap women. In time, after conflicting with their superior officers, the Losers break all convention by engaging the enemy astride Yamaha dirt bikes which are equipped with rocket launchers and machine guns.

While audiences couldn't get enough of the chopper operas, with their exaggerated obnoxiousness and anti-establishment creed, these images were helping create the lowest point in the history of public relations for bikers. Mainstream motorcycle magazines like *Cycle*, *Motorcyclist*, and *Cycle Guide* were at pains to distance the majority of law-abiding, everyday motorcyclists from the images popular on the big screen when they could be bothered to acknowledge the biker movies at all. Letters were commonly appearing in *American Motorcyclist* from riders decrying the effect of so many tough-guy biker movies on a nation's youth. And to a point, they were right. It was, and always has been, a slim margin of the world's motorcyclists who affected the outlaw

image and even fewer the actual lifestyle, but this very vivid minority has long garnered a disproportionate amount of media coverage.

So, just as Brando's *Wild One* had a decade earlier, the outlaw Angels of the 1960s created a myth from which the average Honda-riding commuter on his CB350 or the mature, touring rider who traversed the nation's highways on an Electra Glide would spend years trying to distance themselves. Even the Harley-Davidson Motor Co., the firm responsible for the heavyweight American motorcycles the outlaws saw as the only worthwhile machine, endeavored to under emphasize ties with the types of riders featured in biker movies. A look at Harley-Davidson sales literature and advertisements from the chopper period reveal a company famously out of touch with its core

audience: nary a beard, tattoo, or club insignia in sight.

But the influence of the biker movies throughout the 1960s and 70s could not be denied. Small, aimless groups of Harley riders from all corners of the country saw versions of themselves in the films and started organizing outlaw biker gangs in the best image of the silver screen. An argument could be made that the so-called Big Four outlaw motorcycle gangs would have evolved naturally without the corresponding popularity of the biker movie, but it is worth noting that the Pagans, in Prince George County, Maryland, the Bandidos in Port Arthur, Texas, and the Outlaws in West Palm Beach, Florida, (who faithfully appropriate the Black Rebels Motorcycle Club insignia from *The Wild One* as their club's colors), and,

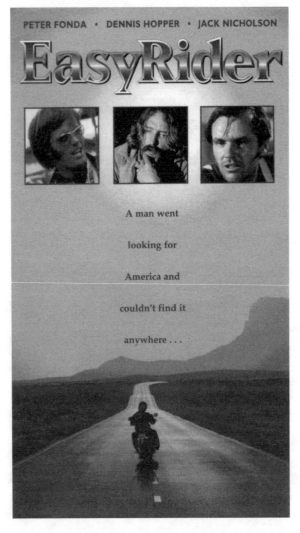

PETER FONDA · DENNIS HOPPER · JACK NICHOLSON

EasyRider

A man went

looking for

America and

couldn't find it

anywhere . . .

of course, the Hell' Angels were profoundly influenced by the biker movies.

Besides the Hell's Angels who had been in existence since the late 1940s, these other three national outlaw biker gangs sprang to prominence between 1965 and 1968—just as *The Wild Angels* and other films brought California's choppers and corresponding grubby outlaw look to mass audiences. And as the outlaw style proliferated in the wake of the biker movie explosion, it was as if the fears of film censors were coming true, with gangs of greasy, ill-tempered yobs just waiting for a movie to come along and offer 90-minute instruction manuals on anti-social behavior.

Brando's smoldering, quietly angry Johnny might have been the biker role model for the 1950s, but when the psychedelic era was in full swing, it was clearly Lee Marvin's boozy court jester Chino that the new generation of bikers most identified with. In time, as the chopper spread from just a West Coast phenomenon to a common sight along Main Street, state legislatures began to adopt more stringent vehicle codes to combat the machines. Spurred on by the opinions of industry safety experts and a mainstream motorcycle press that deemed anything with a rigid frame, springer forks, and no front brake as potentially calamitous as the Hindenburg, the chopper, by the late 1960s, faced possible bureaucratic extinction. In fact, *Run Angel, Run* contains one of the screens first examples of cops using tape measures and state vehicle code books instead of billy clubs to derail a pack of outlaws.

But lawmakers were fighting a stacked deck. There was a growing chopper parts and accessories industry, despite the staggering number of roadside checks and equipment violation citations police departments issued. As the 1960s drew to a close, chopper riders, tired of being ignored by mainstream magazines, had even started their own publications. Most of these magazines were as chintzy as the movies that had helped spread the custom motorcycle trend, mixing a detective magazine's affinity for cheesecake photos with a gearhead's dedication to arcane garage wizardry. *Chopper, Street Chopper*, the briefly published *Colors, Outlaw Biker*, and *F.T.W.* were little more than thinly disguised yearbooks for outlaw bikers. Eventually, with the help of

Out on the road, looking for "the real America," Peter Fonda (center) and Dennis Hopper (left) captured the restlessness of the Flower-Power generation with 1969's *Easy Rider.* (Columbia Tri-Star)

Easyriders magazine, these publications would take the aesthetic from the biker movies to a heretofore unimagined level.

It's difficult to imagine today, some 30 years after their inception, the scandal and embarrassment these publications caused for established motorcycle magazines, even though their readership was very limited initially. But *Easyriders,* which would evolve into a very slick, corporate monthly similar to *Playboy,* was the obvious extension of the 1970 film that bore the same title. For all the seedy, half-hearted efforts that had occurred since Peter Fonda first brought outlaw bikers to prominence to the movies in 1964's *Wild Angels,* it's ironic that it was Fonda who made the final, definitive statement on the period with *Easy Rider.*

Not that filmmakers abandoned the outlaw biker movie after *Easy Rider* (1969). For a while, some saw the international success of the drug-culture classic as a reason to crank out even more biker movies. But the laid-back, spiritual journey

undertaken by Dennis Hopper's Billy and Peter Fonda's Wyatt (or Captain America as his partner refers to him) contained an intellectual and social awareness that pretty much rendered the genre's lesser efforts superfluous. While some critics hailed *Easy Rider* as a masterpiece, others decried it as nothing more than a pot-fueled travelogue of the American Southwest. They're right on both accounts. Where dozens of previous biker movies struggled to maintain fragile plot lines around episodes of violence and road shots, *Easy Rider* was more benign; the two protagonists were only on a search for some intangible "real America." Getting there and avoiding doing anything besides staying stoned along the way were the only items on a tour itinerary as empty as the Arizona hills they traveled through.

Fonda and Hopper's pot-addled riders were clearly not to be lumped in with the countless movie outlaws that preceded them as their languid approach to life was more hippie than Hell's Angel. Instead, this pair use the motorcycle as a

pair of stoned hippie bikers than watching a feature film. Most of all, *Easy Rider* captured the desire many young people had to get out in the world and interpret it their own way, a universal lesson that audiences, bikers or not, could easily relate to. For a film that cost only $340,000 to make, it brought in a staggering $19 million during its initial U.S. release, a huge sum for an independent film in those days.

In time, *Easy Rider* proved so popular it made stars of its creators, including Fonda who co-produced *Easy Rider* and Hopper who proved an adept director. However, it was Jack Nicholson, appearing briefly as an alcoholic young lawyer, whose acting career most benefited from *Easy Rider*. Nicholson told interviewers in 1998 that he'd smoked some 100 joints during production, evident in the sleepy smile he wears for most of his screen time. Even stoned, Nicholson's tragically funny characterization endeared him to audiences, more so than his biker characters had in *Hell's Angels on Wheels* or *Rebel Rousers*. It was as if the filmmakers in *Easy Rider* realized all of the past mistakes limiting the genre and corrected them wholesale: the soundtrack is finally comprised of hip, contemporary rock songs from some of the era's greatest acts, including Steppenwolf, whose title song *Born To be Wild* became the unofficial biker's anthem. Hopper also included a believable LSD trip during the pair's ride to New Orleans, a disturbingly accurate scene that almost made the previous years of bad pot images bearable.

Instead of invading a small town and terrorizing the populace, Captain America and Billy end up being attacked by redneck townies simply for having long hair and "mod" clothes. It was a shockingly sympathetic view of bikers, one that revealed how reviled bikers were by the general public and law enforcement authorities at the time. *Easy Rider* was also notable for including images of the youth culture of which kids could approve. A scene where the wandering pair visit a Colorado hippie commune (where biker movie regular Dan "Grizzly Adams" Haggerty appears as a gentle flower child) was one of the few positive assessments of hippie life on film. Because of this, the commune soon came to replace the isolated rural hamlet as the locale of choice for the

sense of self-expression rather than menace. Captain America and Billy encounter many of the same anti-biker prejudices as other movie motorcyclists, but they'd rather move on than provoke a bloody confrontation. This helped make *Easy Rider* a favorite among people who had never smoked a joint or ridden a chopper. Both actors give memorable performances, with Fonda's introspective role a vivid contrast against Hopper's motor-mouthed wild man. Many are the legends that have sprung up around the scripting of *Easy Rider*, mainly that Hopper's linear, stream-of-consciousness dialogue was improvised. According to the 1996 book of the movie authored by Lee Hill, screenwriter Terry Southern did write most of the film's dialogue. It was Hopper's manic *delivery* that made *Easy Rider* feel more like viewers were eavesdropping on a biker movies that followed *Easy Rider*, including *Angel Unchained* (1970) and later the ridiculously violent *Angels, Hard As They Come* (1971). Both had their gangs invade communes, where the siren call of free love and free pot seemed to lure bikers in against their better judgment.

Easy Rider was presenting its comparatively benign view of chopper riders to the big screen only a few months before TV audiences were to enjoy a similar, positive portrayal of a rebel rider with *Then Came Bronson* (1969). Starring musician-actor Michael Parks, this weekly series caught on with a public who were clearly ready to see bikers portrayed as heroic loners in search of inner peace. Parks sang the series' theme song, *Long, Lonesome Highway*, and launched each of the 26 episodes with a shot of him riding his red Harley Sportster and looking pitifully on a businessman who, unlike Bronson, had a job and responsibilities.

Like *Easy Rider*, *Then Came Bronson* proved a hit with bikers and non-bikers alike for its more believable, if altogether romantic, view of two-wheeled life. Each episode contained some lesson about self-reliance or the hypocrisy of the establishment, while Parks, with a permanent tight-lipped smile on his face, spent a good deal of his screen time riding across some of the prettiest scenery in America. These lengthy road shots that captured the solitude and transcendence of motorcycling were a far cry from the typical negative stereotypes about bikers and probably helped sell more Harley Sportsters than the manufacturers could have realized. There were plenty of motorcyclists who cared little for either of these popular characterizations, but both *Easy Rider* and *Then Came Bronson* were an undeniable step in the right direction and a welcome change of gears after decades of hackneyed images that bikers are still trying to live down.

"Are you gonna stay?"
"Stay? What does that mean?"
Angel (Don Stroud)

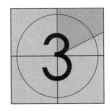

The British Invasion

Mods, Rockers, and Gentleman Marauders

In the days of National Health Service and the full employment that followed the austerity and tight-waisted rationing of WWII, Britain's youths found themselves awash in a never before seen luxury: disposable income. And in a nation with a high regard for motorcycling and motorsports in general, the burgeoning British motorcycle industry claimed a good deal of the estimated annual 500 million pounds burning a hole in teenage pockets.

Converging on the UK at roughly the same time was American rock and roll. A combination of the two resulted in the Rocker cult, a subculture of race-inspired street bikes, black leather, and sneering attitude. Rockers, or youth rebellion in general, provided the basis for a trio of Britain's more interesting biker movies. While only Sidney Furie's *The Leatherboys* (1964) actually utilized the UK's revered transport cafes like the Ace Café (still in operation on the North Circular) as part of its shadowy backdrop, *Some People* (1963) earns merit for offering an in-depth—if not a little exaggerated—view of the underpinnings of the rocker's working-class rebellion.

Both films were undoubtedly inspired by the slew of teenage rebellion and juvenile delinquent exploitation films that had been released to mixed reception in the United States during the 1950s. In Great Britain, the rock and roll fuse was lit in 1954

with the film *Rock Around the Clock,* which caused riots in theaters, followed by a series of well-received concert tours by rockers Gene Vincent, Eddie Cochran and Bill Haley and His Comets. Kids reacted by tearing up concert halls, rioting over a scarcity of tickets and, eventually, forming their own imitation acts.

British filmmakers sought their own answers to James Dean and Marlon Brando, releasing a few lukewarm teen angst films including singer Cliff Richard in *Serious Charge* (1959) and *Expresso Bongo* (1960) a film that explored the whole coffee-bar culture in which the Rockers were to play a prominent role. The UK found its first icon of teen rebellion in pub singer turned teen heartthrob Tommy Hicks who changed his name, greased his hair, and appropriated Elvis' curled lip and hiccuping rockabilly voice in *The Duke Wore Jeans* (1958). British authorities held a strong, reactionary line against youth culture, particularly the potentially corrupting juvenile delinquent films from the United States. Terry "Tex" Childs, a rocker who was a regular both riding and working at the Ace Café during the time, remembers *The Wild One* being banned from distribution in the UK at the time of its 1954 release and staying there for 14 years. (Finland, it is worth noting, also banned *The Wild One* until 1966, but this country's reactionary censors also saw fit to

With the Mods and Rockers fighting at beachside resorts, British filmmaker Sidney J. Furie explored the social conflicts behind his country's rampant youth rebellion in the poignant 1963 drama *The Leatherboys.* **(Allied Artists)**

ban *Abbott and Costello Meet Frankenstein* (1948) for reasons known only to them.)

Regardless of the censors best efforts, the film's anti-authoritarian theme and crazy-cool take on motorcycle clubs was too much for the rockers to resist. "Tex" Childs, while working briefly in the States, brought a copy of *The Wild One* back to the UK to show friends. Apparently, he was not alone: numerous pirated copies were readily available on the underground film circuits in the UK and most members of the rocker-based church charity, the 59 Club, had seen the film at least once by 1960, said Mark Wilsmore, proprietor of the Ace Café.

However successful *The Wild One* was, it still wasn't British. It took *The Leatherboys,* arguably one of the best works to emerge from the whole youth exploitation genre, to make the rocker years known to worldwide audiences. The film's depth can be attributed largely to director Sidney Furie, who brought to the project vast film experience (in 1965 he directed the acclaimed spy thriller *The Ipcress File* with Michael Caine) and legitimacy as a "serious director" who made socially relevant films.

Furie, unlike many sensationalist newspaper editors of the time, seemed to understand the sexual and economic frustrations affecting the rocker phenomenon. The film often depicts motorcycles, and reveals what a necessary role they play in the characters' lives. To these working-class kids, motorcycles were not only daily transportation, but metaphors for their newfound economic and social freedom. When the story's two teenage newlyweds Reggie (Colin Campbell) and Dot (Rita Tushingham) find that a mechanic's meager income doesn't exactly pave a road to marital bliss and a two-bedroom flat in Knightsbridge, the pair begin a series of screaming matches that drive Reggie into the arms of his Triumph motorcycle and, eventually, his best pal Pete, played with irreverent charm by character actor Dudley Sutton.

In stark black and white, Furie captures much of the austere textures of North London, from the cold, foggy night rides the rockers contend with, to the sleek, R.A.F.-inspired black riding leathers they favor. Instead of "battling visigoths," as rockers were depicted in Britain's tabloid press, *The Leatherboys* revealed the rocker's greatest adversary to be money; when Reggie's grandfather dies, deciding who gets the highly desirable free room and board available at his grandparent's home creates one of the film's greatest tensions.

Apparently, Furie's attention to social detail was superior to his knowledge of streetbikes: Rockers from the era say much laughter ensued in theaters during a scene where a tiny Ariel Arrow is shown running alongside Norton Atlases and Triumph Bonnevilles at speed. Despite any technical inaccuracies, *The Leatherboys* contains no shortage of fine action footage. The frigid, typically English weather shows why rockers favored tea to pints (to warm their throttle hands during a ride) while lengthy montages of the gang's road rally to Scotland and back (where each member was required to post a letter to prove having made the 400-mile journey) are among the best riding sequences to be found. The movie also provides a clear glimpse of the early performance bike scene, with the modified café racers and the rocker's obsession with wringing every ounce of speed from their bikes well represented.

Based on a paperback novel from the late 1950s, *The Leatherboys* was considered somewhat shocking at the time, primarily for its tragicomic ending. Tired of his limited life in London, Reggie decides to sell off his bike and relocate to New York with his best mate Pete. But just before departing, Reggie realizes that Pete's close friendship, which served him well during the lengthy and tempestuous disintegration of his marriage, is, as Dot suspected, gay in nature. With many sociologists attempting to label the rockers sexual as well as social deviants, the scene caused an ambivalence about *The Leatherboys* that continues nearly 40 years on. "We loved it because it

Shown here astride a BSA Gold Star café racer in the 1963 biker drama *The Leatherboys*, starlet Rita Tushingham eventually became one of the UK's most respected actresses. (Allied Artists)

showed us the Ace and the lads doing The Ton," remembers "Tex" Childs, who can still be found doling out tea and chips at the re-opened café today. "Nobody cared much for the mushy parts." Obviously, the censors agreed, granting *The Leatherboys* an X rating which almost guaranteed its box office failure.

It is worth noting how Furie skirted the Rockers' much-ballyhooed dealings with their subculture nemesis, the Mods. These two groups constituted the largest youth subcultures in Britain at the time, with the Rockers hailing from working-class backgrounds with a taste for vintage rock and roll and fast motorbikes. The Mods were the larger group who tended to come from more affluent homes and favored Italian scooters, Air Force parkas, and "Mod" pop music. *The*

Black leather, Brylcreem and bad attitudes were the order of the day in *Some People*, a 1963 British release that sensationalized the problems of working class bikers in the industrial center of Bristol. (American International Pictures)

Leatherboys was released in the summer of 1964, during the peak year of the two groups' massive seaside brawls at Brighton, Blackpool, and Margate, but nowhere in the film is reference made to the Mod's dreaded "hair dryers" (Vespa scooters).

By ignoring the most violent aspects of youth culture, it seems that British "motorcycle hoodlums," as they were called in the press, generally received a far better treatment on film than their American counterparts would a few years later during the peak years of stateside biker exploitation films. Screen the entire run of 1960s Hell's Angels movies and nowhere will you find sympathetic images of a biker's homelife or bids to offer social explanations for their anti-social behavior. Talking with rockers hanging around the Ace today offers something of an explanation: they claim the often soft-edged portrayal of rockers in movies is at least partly due to a tolerance of, if not outright acceptance of, the Ton Up Boys by the general public. Most Britons viewed them as a certifiable nuisance, but also as crazy kids who would eventually cut their hair, take white collar jobs, vote Tory, and generally come 'round. In a country where former roadracers like Geoff Duke and John Surtees were lionized by the public, the rockers' greatest transgression, a devotion to fast riding—albeit on public roads—was considered more annoying than terrifying.

Of course, there were millions of everyday motorcyclists throughout the United Kingdom who felt the cinema's fixation on the rockers and "bad" motorcyclists was short shrift of the first order. The mainstream motorcycle press and the majority of riders felt the biker movies were unjustly portraying motorcyclists with negative stereotypes, and rightly so. England's tabloid dailies were rife with headlines about "motorcycle hoodlums" and "two-wheeled Vikings." Labels like these did little to advance the image of the country's motorcycle industry and even less for respectable riders who had never even seen a rocker before. Both *The Leatherboys,* and *Some People* were made during the peak years of the British motorcycle industry's dominance of racing, but nowhere is racing mentioned in either of these films. From the 1950s with British racing superiority through the 1960s and 70s with Mike Hailwood and Phil Read, national pride in grand prix champions was at a fever pitch. However, against the sordid, melodrama of teen rebellion, competition riding always lost out when movie producers went looking for subject matter. A racer and serious adult motorcycle enthusiast is quoted in Johnny Stuart's excellent period study, *Rockers* as being "sick and tired of reading about a load of layabouts who never traveled farther than the local coffee bar. . . I've been riding motorcycles for 32 years and I consider myself an enthusiast, unlike the morons who call themselves 'rockers.'" Letters like these, written by law abiding riders no doubt sick of their neighbors suddenly perceiving their motorcycles as sinister and anti-social, filled the editorial pages of newspapers and enthusiast publications like *Motor Cycle News* in the wake of films like *The Leatherboys*, just as they would when U.S. studios proffered its Hell's Angels films a few years later.

Less sympathetic than *The Leatherboys*, but no less topical, was the motorcycle espionage-science-fiction movie *These Are The Damned* (1961). Starring an unbelievably young Oliver Reed as King, this Joseph Losey film was an unashamed attempt to play upon every societal ill and bogey man lurking in Britain's closet during the Cold War years. Though *These Are The Damned* was a fairly large-budget film produced by America's Columbia Pictures Corporation, and while it may have offered a few frights and thrills for postwar British audiences, when viewed today the movie is about as stiff as a day-old fish and chips wrapper. For instance, King's gang, replete with DA haircuts, black leather jackets, and a peculiar habit of walking in step as if their moves had been choreographed, spends its afternoons in the seaside resort of Weymouth making trouble for the locals and tourists. Reed as King, for some untold reason, appears dressed in a tweed blazer and necktie, looking less like a rocker or switchblade-wielding Teddy Boy than a public school cricket player. American soap opera legend Macdonald Carey appears as Simon Wells, a vacationing insurance executive who inevitably ends up getting beaten and robbed by the rocker gang. Minutes later, Wells utters the unforgettable line, "I never expected a thing like this to happen to me in England." "You thought England was a land of old ladies knitting socks. The age of senseless violence is upon us too," comes the reply.

These Are The Damned has serious pretensions, but ends up falling flat from a recurring case of the overdramatics. For instance, when King's sister Joanie (Shirley Anne Field) runs off with Wells to escape the brutal life of the rocker gang, Wells quickly attempts to lecture her about the merits of respectable, middle-class life. It must have worked, because in a few hours they decide to marry. The movie's serious, romantic tone is then undermined by one of the silliest theme songs from any youth rebellion film ever made. Curiously, the rocker gang picks up the melody several times, whistling and singing along like extras from *West Side Story*. And just when *These Are The Damned* seems secured into the familiar patterns of *working class kids gone wrong* films, the entire cast soon find themselves awash on a remote (is there any other kind) island where a secret government cabal is conducting bizarre experiments on a group of orphans.

If the concept of hyper-intelligent children possessing unusual powers sounds familiar, it should. A very similar theme was used with the white-eyed mutant toddlers in *Village of the Damned*, a classic piece of British science fiction from two years earlier. But unlike the earlier film, *These Are The Damned* never fully explains what's so scary about radioactive children designed by Defense Department operatives; instead, they just sit around and whine about "feeling funny."

While the science-fiction theme falls flat, Oliver Reed's taut intensity plays well against the

> "I never expected a thing like this to happen to me in England."
> "You thought England was a land of old ladies knitting socks. The age of senseless violence is upon us too."
> *These Are The Damned*

If Viveca Lindfors thinks this biker gang is scary, wait until she encounters a group of radioactive children living in a secret government compound. Atomic Age horror meets the greaser set in *These Are The Damned* (1963). (Hammer Films Productions, LTD)

otherwise tranquil cast. Moody and sullen, he is easily the best aspect of this movie. The gang uses King's (Reed's) sister Joanie (Viveca Lindfors) to lure tourists into alleys where they're promptly beaten and robbed, and Reed at times appears so intent on destroying someone or something, that he makes the threat of radioactive offspring seem attractive by comparison. With its creepy nuclear secrets, marauding gangs of angry, confused teenagers, and scores of unwanted children at every turn, *These Are The Damned* reads like a week of headlines from *The Daily Mirror*, circa 1962. Motorcycles, in this case, a half-dozen basically stock-looking Triumph Bonnevilles and Speed Twins, play a relatively small role, serving more as a universal symbol of youthful rebellion than a manifestation of the newfound mobility and freedom of British youth. The film does contain one good, extended riding sequence where the Rockers run a brief race through the streets of Weymouth, buzzing through traffic roundabouts

as if they're on the Brand's Hatch Superbike circuit. At one point, King, riding without a helmet, even manages to lock up the ineffective drum brakes on his old Triumph twin—no easy feat, even for a stuntman! Overall, *These Are The Damned* is an interesting period piece, even though it could only be classified as a biker movie for its first half-hour. Overdrawn and too serious for its own good, the movie never seems to decide which of it's three genres it intends to represent.

A fairer, almost social worker's perspective on the rocker rebellion was covered by *Some People*, the 1963 movie that, like *The Leatherboys* and the class-conscious BBC youth drama *Up The Junction* (1967) provides a non-judgmental look at the daily lives of the then-dreaded bike boys. Full of sullen glances, curled-lipped insolence and second-rate, homemade rock music, *Some People* draws its title from the film's central theme of some people being able to follow orders and fit in, while some others cannot. Lucky for viewers. The

Desperate to add fire to the biker gang movie formula, *Psychomania* (1971), attempted to shock audiences with a mix of 1960s psychedelia and tales of the occult. (Benmar Productions, LTD)

non-conformity at the movie's core is classic bad-boy stuff, lending both insight and exaggeration to the working of the juvenile delinquent mind.

Filmed in color in the booming industrial city of Bristol, *Some People* focuses, like *The Leatherboys*, more on the sociological side of rocker life, choosing to use motorcycles only intermittently; both ends of the film are filled with images of some wonderful period café racers, but you'll have to look closely to discern makes and models. British viewers might find it amusing that some 40 years after *Some People* was filmed, the rocker era seems a period of relative innocence. Only one scene is shot in a pub and there the rockers are disgusted by the drunkenness of their fathers' generation. Other drugs, too, are non-existent in this film. Even the slogans and images the riders use to decorate their black leather jackets are innocuous, ranging from motorcycle manufacturer's logos to American cartoon characters like Yogi Bear.

Some People contains a few minutes of spirited street riding, though its best café racing sequence is marred by some truly poor editing. The herky-jerky film cuts unintentionally make a dangerous crash look hilarious and obviously staged. After being nicked by police for racing on public roads, John (Kenneth Moore), Beeza Bill (David Andrews), and Bert (David Hemmings) find themselves banned from road riding for a year, a sentence akin to being forced to ride a scooter for eternity to any respecting Ton Up Boy. A judge delivers a lecture to the pair which summed up much of what the establishment disliked about rockers: "When you young chaps buy these powerful machines, you have in your hands a most dangerous weapon. I think it's most monstrous that mere boys like you should be able to buy these things so cheaply and easily." Any bike

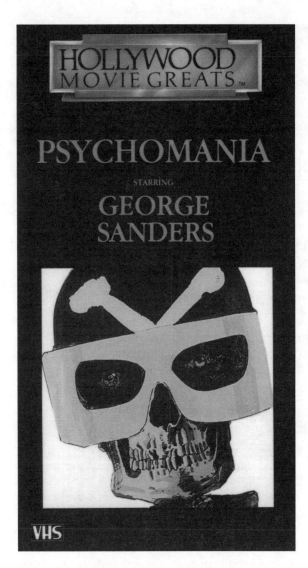

interest in things outside the transport cafes and performance-tuning his Triumph 650, the tall and gangly Bill, in the best tradition of juvenile delinquents everywhere, refuses to comply. Bill resents his former bike mate's upper-class pretensions about "going it straight," and spends the entire second half of the film with his head slunk between his shoulders like an angry vulture.

Inevitably, John is dumped by the upper-crust Ann when she leaves for college, and, apparently, a higher class of friends and boyfriends. Soon John reconciles with his rocker pals who appear to have been hanging around the local chip shop, posing in their leather riding suits all the while. John, torn between two worlds, watches tight-lipped as Bill and his rocker friends tear apart the youth hall where he'd been meeting with his "straight" friends. Unlike the pat, resolute, happy ending of American films that always sought to teach youths that crime and non-conformity does not pay, *Some People* appears calculated to reinforce in viewers the pointlessness of attempting to transcend their class-structure. Like the popular "After School Specials" from ABC TV, there's plenty of heavy-handed message-mongering in Britain's motorcycle rebellion films. The filmmakers make it clear that the lads regard their motorbikes and the rocker identity as a relief from the dead-end jobs and mortgages of their parent's generation. The filmmakers are careful to fill *Some People* with multiple images of Bristol's industrial sector, inferring that jobs were available for good boys willing to play by the rules. So when the rockers choose to continually screw up any opportunity to better themselves, they are in effect poking a finger in the eye of respectability by rejecting the spirit-killing jobs that life seems to have deigned for them. Even an evening at the pub with John's dad doesn't go very well—the younger man can't stand to see his old man drunk and dispirited by life, and runs off to avoid what looks like his own inevitable future. Heavy stuff to be ingested by your average early 60s teenager, but *Some People*'s stark themes make an interesting lesson in British class structure and an enjoyable biker movie.

Rockers also found their way onto BBC television during the early 1960s, and not only through

rider who has ever been on the receiving end of a traffic ticket will recognize the tenor of this speech. However, there's an option available to the lads which will allow them to clear their names from the list of banned motorcyclists, and that's to enroll in *and* complete one of the Duke of Edinburgh's Youth Training Schemes. These public service programs were aimed at curing teens of youthful irresponsibility through charity work and adventure, though their effectiveness has long been debated. The bikers, of course, only want to ride again, so they quickly accept a youth warden's challenge to straighten up in order to get their bikes back on the road. Bereft of riding, they dive headfirst into forming a rock band with Ann, the warden's respectable, and highly hairsprayed daughter. But as John develops an news broadcasts for their exploits in street brawls and spectacular crashes. An episode of the weekly detective series *Dixon of Dock Green* centered around the peculiar and dangerous habit of "record racing" which was briefly popular at the country's numerous transport cafes. Speed-crazed riders would often choose a quick-paced rock and roll record on a juke box and then challenge the clock by racing to a pre-determined point and back before the record had finished. Record racing made for spectacular headlines, as did the Mods/Rockers brawls that provide the nexus of *Crazy Baby*, an ultra low-budget Italian-German co-production that's laughably as bad as any Ed Wood stinker. With dialogue dubbed so poorly it brings to mind those out-of-synch vocalizations from Japanese monster movies, *Crazy Baby* is the kind of movie that could be shown at hospitals for the clinically depressed as a sure-fire laugh-maker.

Even the "brawl" between Mods and Rockers is half-hearted; the "rockers" are actually five shadowy figures on what appear to be WWII-era Harley side-valve 45s. Dressed in U.S. war surplus, they look like extras from TV's *Rat Patrol*. Faring little better is Italian pop singer Ricky Shane as the central mod hero, Shane, who claims to have "fought for his life every Saturday night," plays his wandering troubadour with hairy-chested aplomb. It's tough to watch a star vehicle for a star you've never heard of, and *Crazy Baby's* billing as a motorcycle movie is the biggest ruse of all. After the initial encounter with the chain-wielding Rockers at the Liverpool pub (which, suspiciously, is filled with bottles of Grappa and advertising signs written entirely in Italian) there's barely a motorcycle or even motor scooter to be found for the remainder of the film.

Instead, we're treated to 90 minutes of Shane smooching with Italian beauties and singing his cornball pop tunes in bohemian cafes. Labeling

> "When you young chaps buy these powerful machines, you have in your hands a most dangerous weapon. I think it's most monstrous that mere boys like you should be able to buy these things so cheaply and easily."
> Court Judge
> *Some People*

this turkey a biker movie, with all the production quality of an amateur porno flick, is about as misguided as calling Quentin Tarantino's *Reservoir Dogs* wholesome family entertainment. But *Crazy Baby*, which could have been titled "Elvis Goes Italian," does reveal how archetypal the Rocker had become, especially when European filmmakers needed a convenient screen villain.

By the late 1960s, the British cinema had largely turned its back on the biker movie, mainly because the country's youth had moved on to other things. The idea of working class kids beating holy hell out of each other because of fashion choices or the types of transportation they chose seemed as silly to a new generation of teenagers as it had to adults a few years earlier. The Mods and Rockers were soon replaced by hippies, skinheads and Hell's Angels, bringing with them their own rebellion, fashion, and, eventually, films.

With flower power, woman's rights, and worldwide peace protests over Vietnam, British filmmakers in the 1970s all but excised the motorcyclist from the roster of themes to draw on for inspiration, with one exception.

Psychomania (1971), proved that when simple youth violence no longer sold tickets, youth violence peppered with a vampire-zombie formula just might fill a few seats. The story of gangs of wayward teens transforming into monsters is as old as *I Was A Teenage Werewolf*. These kinds of films were always over-the-top campy, like dramatizations of a high school guidance counselor's nightmares. They also reveal much about how parents really feel about their tough-to-understand kids.

In *Psychomania* the biker gang, appropriately named The Living Dead, is classic troublemaking youth gone bad. When they tire of racing each other through the streets and terrorizing shoppers by riding through a pedestrian mall, they opt for a mass-suicide which gang leader Tom, played with an absolute dedication to drollery by Nicky Henson, believes will lend them special powers. It does, and those powers arrive namely in a newfound ability to drive headlong against traffic, daring motorists to, well, kill them. But wait—Tom, and his fellow gang members cannot be killed because they're already dead. This realization becomes an open invitation to all sorts of two-wheeled hijinks.

The Living Dead ride the usual assortment of partially customized Triumphs, bikes which, in one scene, develop a miraculous ability to ride over rocky turf without wiping out. The bikes are also adept at bumping off enemies of the club, either indoors or out. And oddly, whenever a victim falls to one of the zombie bikes, there's precious little blood or evidence of injury. The Living Dead also favor really goofy helmets which sport Plexiglas face-shields decorated with giant skulls. The effect is about as menacing as a Martha Stewart luncheon and just as pretentious.

What makes *Psychomania* such a product of the times and so different from the previous British biker movies was the lack of social conscience. Instead of class conflict and working-man's angst, there's half-baked mysticism and hippie spirituality that affected so many films during the 1970s. There are unintelligible metaphors for evil involving a reappearing frog and too many candlelight seances. There's also a neo-Stonehenge monolith that somehow fuels the gang's supernatural activities. And *Psychomania's* screenplay contains enough stilted dialogue to suggest there must have been an extended writer's strike in Britain during 1971. Some saw *Psychomania* as the low-tide for British motorcycle movies, and it would be madness to argue with them. The British made few biker movies over the next decade, but the country was producing few films of any kind during an extended economic recession. That recession would eventually decimate the country's motorcycle industry as well, with vaunted marquees Triumph, BSA, and Norton all ceasing production during the 1970s and early '80s.

There was one moment of movie brilliance with *Quadrophenia* (1979). The nearly two-hour movie was released to critical acclaim, and for good reason. It's not often that movies about motorcycling subcultures are given such top-flight treatment. The film is helped along by the screen premiere of musician-actor Sting (as the ultra-suave Ace, king of the Mods) and exemplary acting from Phil Daniels as Jimmy. *Quadrophenia*, a word meant to imply a person with four distinct personalities, uses a screenplay derived from the accompanying double album by The Who. The band was emerging from the Mod scene in the early 60s, and Daltrey, Moon, Entwistle, and Townsend served as executive producers as well as script consultants using many of their personal experiences in the film. Like *Some People* and *The Leatherboys* before it, *Quadrophenia* studies youth rebellion through a filter of social struggle and class identity. But with 16 years of hindsight at director Franc Roddam's disposal, a more cognizant and less romantic look at a too-often lionized period emerges.

At the center is Jimmy, a wiry and typically angry teenager who, despite his family's inauspicious Eastender background, is making his way in the business world as an up-and-coming mail clerk. He's fully expected to launch himself out of the family's cold water flat—that is, unless his affiliation with his Mod buddies doesn't produce other results. Jimmy has an acute sense of his own place in history, carefully clipping newspaper accounts of the Mod's seaside brawls and indulging himself deeper and deeper into the Mods' group identity. This obsession with being part of the in-crowd, from wearing an oversized green parka covered in buttons, to riding a Lambretta scooter and popping enough pills to give Timothy Leary a seizure, leads to Jimmy's inevitable disillusionment.

Along the way, *Quadrophenia* shows what life must have really been like at the time. Its smartly written screenplay, which, like the album that inspired it, questions whether there was ever anything more to these two cults than the empowerment and thrill of belonging, is best illustrated in a hilarious scene at the public baths where Jimmy and a Rocker engage in a contest to drown out each other's singing. When the two realize that the fellow in the next tub is an old school chum, each now straddling different sides of the pop culture spectrum, Jimmy and his old friend Kevin are faced with deciding whether to mock convention by becoming friends again.

Choosing his Mod buddies over his old friend is one of many bad decisions Jimmy makes, including losing his job, getting arrested, and being thrown out of the house. Previously absent from British biker movies, drugs make a big appearance here, with the Mods openly ingesting hundreds of blue amphetamine tabs in order to stay up all night for dance parties. Period music from Booker T and the MG's, The Ronettes, and other 60s soul artists favored by the original Mods is interspersed with The Who's own narrative tunes with great effect. Part of the ritual of Mod and Rocker life was to ride their machines mostly at night, after work, and Roddam smartly chooses to shoot many scenes in near dark; the edgy gloom adds to the sense of youthful urgency.

Fans of motor scooters and motorcycles alike have plenty to cheer about in *Quadrophenia*, with the pitched street fights all being conducted via two-wheelers. For some reason, the Rockers are often filmed riding without helmets, and many of the Triumph and BSA café racers sport tall, chopper-style handlebars, unheard-of in the 1960s. The technical inconsistencies may just be dictated by the film's being shot in 1979: a scene where the two gangs converge along the Brighton Promenade for a punch-up contains an embarrassing shot of a movie theater marquee advertising *Heaven Can Wait,* a movie shown in theaters 16 years after the Brighton rumbles took place. Not to be missed is a hilarious segment where Jimmy and several Mod friends are unable to find a place to sleep during the Brighton weekend, and end up crashing in a boat-storage alcove along the shore. In the dark they stumble over several snoring bodies, only to learn upon awakening that their bedmates are a gang of Rockers. Though *Quadrophenia* never culled massive box-office figures in the UK or Stateside, the film has proven popular with both fans of The Who and British motorcycle buffs. It also spawned a musical stage production in 1999, which enjoyed a healthy run on London's West End. Moreover, *Quadrophenia* proves that biker movies don't have to be low-budget or lowbrow.

To say these films have developed a cult following in the UK would be an understatement of the first order. Though virtually unknown to American audiences, *The Leatherboys,* for instance,

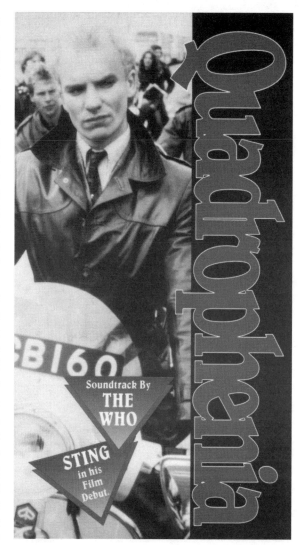

has inspired organized motorcycling tours past the sites where scenes were filmed. The title *These Are The Damned* was appropriated by the legendary punk rock band of the same name, led by Dave Vanian, a Rocker and member of the vaunted 59 Club. Recreations of clothing worn by the Rockers in *Some People* are available new from specialty catalogs in the UK. It goes without saying that Britain's motorcycling heritage is far deeper than, and cannot be accurately surmised by, a small batch of films about the brief-lived Rocker phenomenon, despite the lasting effects 1960s youth culture had on British cinema. A small number of well-made and accurate films about competition riding have trickled out of

JONATHAN DEMME PRESENTS

EAT THE PEACH

"'Eat The Peach' is the best motorcycle movie since 'Easy Rider,' and the funniest ever."
David Sterritt, CHRISTIAN SCIENCE MONITOR

Bridges and Brit pop star David Essex proved a hit with racing fans, while Ireland, a country with its own rich motorcycling heritage (but no motorcycle films to speak of) released the art house classic *Eat The Peach* in 1986. Slowly paced and filled with characteristic Irish understatement, *Eat The Peach* is one of the most human motorcycling stories ever filmed. Like the 1970 US release, *Little Fauss and Big Halsy, Peach* chronicles the hard-luck tale of a pair of traveling motorcycle enthusiasts. They first lose their jobs when their Japanese employers pull up stakes, and then, like so many others, have their lives changed after watching an Elvis Presley movie, *Roustabout*. Watching the film prompts a brainstorm: the two decide to erect one of those old wooden Wall of Death thrill rides which uses centrifugal force to run bikes against gravity's pull.

Director Peter Ormond works from a true story and all the lumps and bumps of a low-level motorcycle daredevil's life are clearly represented. Eamon Morrissey as Arthur and the perpetually sad-faced Stephan Brennan as Vinnie are driven to restore their injured pride (not to mention knees, backs, etc.) with the rickety sideshow attraction, though things never work out as planned. The often morose, but sometimes funny *Eat The Peach* is a low-fidelity masterpiece, similar to Bill Forsythe's sleepy Scottish comedy *Local Hero* (1983) in pacing and in its careful character study. Arthur and Vinnie are in a constant contest to keep their vintage Harley 45's in functioning order. Gasoline in the small, perpetually misty Irish villages where they perform is either of questionable octane or just plain unavailable. Overall, *Eat The Peach,* which has proven a cable TV hit in recent years, seems more focused on teaching audiences about the importance of maintaining faith in one's dreams than any sort of statement on rebellion. This makes it a success as biker movies go, unearthing a side of motorcycling seldom approached in the movies.

Unfortunately, *Eat The Peach* was the last bike film to emerge from the British Isles in many years. At the end of the 20th century it's almost as if the British have entirely ceased producing motorcycle films. It's worth noting that the only motorcycle feature produced in two decades is another Rocker flick, this time, the 12-minute

Great Britain since the 1930s, and are discussed further in Chapter 4.

What the early British biker movies have in common with their later, youth-rebellion counterparts is a dedication to broad story lines and subplots involving the ever-present class struggles. Though *No Limit* (1935) was basically a screwball musical comedy that just happened to use the Isle of Man TT races as a backdrop, the following film, *Once a Jolly Swagman* (1938) was fully socially aware. A slow trickle of biker movies emerged from England in the 1980s and, though few in number, showed a marked improvement from the low-budget teen exploitation films of the 1960s. The grand prix racing drama *Silver Dream Racer* (1980) starring American actor Beau video *Tunnel of Love* (1998). The brief, black-and-white film is scored by former Clash frontman Joe Strummer and because of its reliance on quick edits and music, plays almost like an extended music video. Many saw the piece as a vanity project for filmmaker Robert Milton Wallace which stars model Tamara Beckwith and stunt ace Eddie Kidd. Others saw it as proof that the Rocker film, loved by the café racer crowd and reviled by much of society, remains the archetypal British biker movie.

Full Throttle

Off to the Races

During my first visit to the banked track at Daytona's International Speedway, I remember being struck by two things: the sheer size and scale was undeniably awe-inspiring, and the sights and sounds of a pack of roadracers zipping along the 30-degree banked turns looked curiously similar to a scene from a movie. But unfortunately for the world's motorcycle enthusiasts, that movie has never made it to the screen. That filmmakers have continually ignored motorcycle racing as a subject for films is a missed opportunity of the first order. Screenwriters have overlooked what is arguably the most exciting and broad aspect of motorcycling where countless dramatic possibilities, involving everything from the personal struggles of competitors to the pit-lane technological improvisations of race team crews, remain virtually untapped.

Besides the undeveloped photogenic possibilities of Daytona, other circuits around the world offer similarly breathtaking possibilities, not the least of which is the vaunted 38-mile mountain circuit on the Isle of Man off the coast of Ireland. As the world's longest-running continuous road race, the Isle of Man's Tourist Trophy (or TT) held each spring is a feature-length screenplay waiting to happen. The tiny Manx island is rife with ruggedly beautiful natural scenery and an unforgiving race course comprised mainly of public roads

through towns and villages. Claiming the lives of several racers each year since its 1907 inception, the TT race has only once captured the imagination of a filmmaker, British director Monty Banks.

When Banks launched *No Limit* in 1934, the Isle of Man TT was already renowned throughout Europe as a race course where only the bravest automobile and motorcycle racers would compete. The annual event was drawing tens of thousands of competitors to the otherwise quiet island, an event Banks couldn't resist as a backdrop for a romantic racing comedy. In the lead role is veteran Vaudeville star George Formby, a popular British comedian who had perfected a characterization of a gap-toothed, relatively luckless everyman with which most Britons could easily identify. Formby's George Shuttleworth plays nearly every scene for laughs, contorting his mule-face and lanky frame like a cartoon character, but there's an underlying current of reality in *No Limit* that must have been recognizable to thousands of TT enthusiasts.

Formby, the quintessential privateer, has concocted his checkerboard racer, christened The Shuttleworth Snap, in his family's tiny home garage. Shuttleworth has squandered most of his earnings from his job as a chimney sweep and all of his attentions on a pipe dream of racing against what was already a well-funded roster of factory racers. Up against Nortons, Ariels, Triumphs, and others from the then-strong stable of British motorcycle manufacturers, Formby doesn't even have money for the ferry to cross the Irish Sea to the Isle of Man. Instead, he plays on pluck, wit, and his ability to corral throngs of travelers to hear his warbling ballads about his race aspirations, played to nerve-wracking effect on a mandolin. Like racers since the TT's inception, Formby's character is so hyped about competing on the fabled mountain course that he seems relatively unconcerned about the inherent dangers of racing around sheer cliffs and through populated towns. And, following in true privateer tradition, Shuttleworth is clearly the odd man out with better-equipped, better-trained factory riders barely giving him consideration as a serious competitor. Formby's bike, which manages to set a new course record by having its throttle stick open during practice—is actually an AJS side-valve 350, its distinctive single-cylinder pop-pop-pop exhaust note recognizable to vintage racing fans. The bike's full fairing resembles the bodywork from an old Sopwith Camel bi-plane, another of *No Limit's* interesting effects, mirroring the early dustbin fairings that would see action on the Isle in years to come.

With all the clumsy luck of Bugs Bunny, Shuttleworth shows up at the TT just seconds before the race begins. He can't race, however, because this talented-but-bumbling amateur has accepted a bribe from a competing factory bigwig not to enter. A last-minute change of heart sees Shuttleworth, dressed nattily in a vintage racing outfit of baggy brown leathers and pudding bowl helmet, skidding, crashing, and, with the throttle stuck open on his borrowed Ariel Red Hunter 350, somehow managing to best the competition. Even with the relatively limited film technology available at the time, director Banks manages to capture some thrilling race footage, including some of the first at-speed footage of motorcycles on the TT circuit. The movie's stunts—and there are plenty, including a racer crashing through a pub, a blown engine catching fire, and several gnarly pile-ups—were performed by members of the Island's Manx Motor Cycle Club. The competition riders, already familiar with the intricacies of the difficult TT circuit, were hired on to film the extensive racing scenes after a Canadian stunt team backed out, due to the inherent dangers of the TT circuit.

With riders bursting through fence posts, into each other, and over hillsides, *No Limit* pulls no punches when dramatizing the potential pratfalls of the TT course, and the shots are still enough to lift viewers off their bar stools some 65 years later. Similarly, *No Limit* provides a fascinating view of the TT circuit's familiar points—from the downhill hairpin at Governor's Bridge to the winding village roads past stone pubs and cottages to the misty, mountain sweepers at Windy Corner—all with surprising clarity. True to his hapless form, Shuttleworth finds his nearest competitors, the rival Sprocket team, conspiring to make him crash out of the race. After nearly kissing the walls of a dozen or so corners and being kicked and shoved all over the course, Shuttleworth's mishaps turn golden as he winds up finishing the course with not only first place, but the affections of Florence Desmond, played, (and how's this for an early product placement) by a real-life Team Rainbow factory girl. To this day, fans are unsure whether *No Limit* was intended by London's A.T.P. Studios to be interpreted as a musical, a comedy, or an action picture. Nevertheless, it's one of the only feature films ever made on a subject and location that could easily yield dozens more.

Where *No Limit* only hinted at the overwhelming class and money conflicts prevalent in international roadracing, Britain's next racing film, the excellent *Once a Jolly Swagman* (1948) takes on social issues so firmly, the film's conscience nearly overshadows the racing. As with Formby's George Shuttleworth, Bill Fox, played with stodgy coolness by a young Dirk Bogarde, is an unknown bumpkin who appears at the track looking to have a go. Fox, a bored glassworks factory laborer, has no money, few credentials and doesn't even arrive with his own racing leathers. What he has in overabundance is ambition which he reveals to an opportunistic race team manager, Lag Gibbon (played by Bill Owen,) after a few laps around the dirt oval Speedway track. Speedway was a forerunner of American flat-track racing, a quarter-mile dirt oval track race using four-stroke 500cc singles of various makes. The bikes were equipped with one gear, narrow tires, and, in an inspired moment of engineering sadism, no brakes. Teams of four riders competed in each race, steering the bikes sideways for much of the track, tossing up brilliant rooster tails of dirt, and, occasionally, each other.

Needless to say, these exhibitions of sheer nerve proved a popular draw with audiences throughout the UK and Europe in the 1920s and 30s. The races, which are still run today on ice and dirt, drew their largest, most enthusiastic crowds in the WWII era where the movie is set. *Once a Jolly Swagman,* derived from a French novel by Montagu Slater, reveals how the racers were a group of relatively innocent thrill-seekers who often ended up losing everything to satisfy popular demand. The avaricious, cigar-chomping Lag Gibbon sees lots of potential and pound signs in the young Bill Fox, who's only concerned with the need to run ever faster lap times. Fox starts out happy just to be on the track at all, but after watching some of his fellow riders injured rather horribly and compensated very poorly for their pains, he starts to rethink his priorities. In fact, about fifteen minutes into *Once a Jolly Swagman,* viewers are treated to a set-up for Fox's unrelenting demands for a racer's union: his unforgiving factory foreman sacks him for missing an afternoon of work, and the point is driven home in the best propaganda tradition by depicting the factory as a spirit-crushing den of tedium. Undeterred in his quest for fair treatment—and after his working-class family reminds young Fox that they can't afford to support him without a job—the idealistic Fox takes after the ruling economic hierarchy of racing like Vladimir Lenin himself. The film, as Sidney Furie's *The Leatherboys* and *Quadrophenia* would decades later, is not afraid to mix important, social issues with motorcycling; the veteran speedway racers are depicted as hard-drinking, burned-out hacks who've soured on fan expectations, frequent injuries and bad pay.

Despite its obvious cant toward Labor Party politics, *Swagman* remains a racing film for most of its 100-minute duration. The on-track scenes contain some of the best racing footage ever filmed, with fantastic, track-level camera angles and close-ups of the riders' faces adding to the tension. At a time when most movie directors were content to simply posit actors and machines in front of a moving picture screen and simulate movement, director Jack Lee created a technique that places viewers startlingly close to the action. Extensive nighttime scenes shot at London's New Cross Speedway involve thousands of extras, and Lee manages to fully capture the apprehension of veteran riders and the soccer-game enthusiasm of the anthem-singing crowds. Unlike *No Limits,* *Swagman* is a fully modern film incorporating many high-speed camera techniques that would later become the industry standards. It was considered a large-budget film for its time, receiving widespread distribution throughout the UK and Europe. The film's sometimes heavy-handed political bent didn't affect its admirable box-office draw, with fans of speedway and Bogarde showing up in equal numbers. *Once a Jolly Swagman* (which refers to a nickname the riders coined) accurately depicts its speedway racers sitting out a hiatus during Britain's involvement in WWII. When the war is over, Fox is still embroiled in his struggle for union representation at the track. He's managed to alienate his family and his fellow racers and has lost sight of the importance of simple competition, perhaps intended as a lesson to racers to concentrate on pole position, not politics.

The war that interrupted the racing in *Once a Jolly Swagman* also suspended nearly all forms of motorsports around the world for more than six years. When racing resumed in the late 1940s, movie directors had moved on to other subjects, perhaps forgetting the ready-made dramatics that motorcycle racing provided. It's a shame no directors or producers found interest in what was to be the classic era of motorcycle racing. In the US, legends were being made at the Daytona 200, an annual event gaining mainstream popularity. In Europe, legendary Italian motorcycle racer Giacomo Agostini and the UK's Geoff Duke, John Surtees, and Mike Hailwood were setting track records, thrilling audiences, and bringing the sport of motorcycling to millions of new fans.

Still, the movie cameras stayed away.

Intermittent coverage of international road and dirt races made it to television and ABC's Wide World of Sports occasionally broadcast stunt rider Evel Knievel's bigger jumps. But as for feature-length films, motorcycle competition had

MOTORCYCLE SPORT AND THE MEN WHO RIDE ON ANY SUNDAY

A FILM BY BRUCE BROWN

Featuring Mert Lawwill, Malcolm Smith and Steve McQueen.

it a point to show up at the AMA's road racing meets, like the Loudon Classic in Laconia, New Hampshire, but few, if any, bothered to take in the goings-on at the track. Similarly polarized were professional racers who lived in a world where the term *modified motorcycle* meant not the raked-out, kaleidoscopic choppers from popular films, but big-inch race motors in purpose-built lightweight frames.

It wasn't until a booming US economy in the 1960s fostered a sales surge in motorcycles that a young surfer, motorcyclist, and filmmaker, named Bruce Brown created a movie with which competition riders could identify. After two decades of suffering through *The Wild Angels,* both on screen and off, dominating the public's perception of motorcycling, it's hard to overestimate the relief motorcyclists must have felt when *On Any Sunday* (1971) was released to theaters. The 90-minute color documentary, which Brown wrote, produced, and directed, was such a shot in the arm to two-wheeled sports that the United Nations awarded Brown's work as Outstanding American Film for 1971. Mainstream media outlets from the *San Francisco Examiner* to the *New York Times,* who had long written off motorcycling as the sole province of perverts, thugs, and druggies, lined up to heap praise on Brown's film, with critics describing it as both "remarkably gentle" and "thrilling." They were right. Brown's year spent collecting footage for his film was put to good use as he managed to create what is basically an eloquent advertisement for the sport of motorcycling. And instead of simply focusing on its more sensational aspects, *On Any Sunday* presents motorcycling as both a hobby for everyday families and a serious vocation for trained professionals.

On Any Sunday is scored with plenty of breezy, instrumental pop tunes, which carry slow-motion footage of dirt bikers roosting over sand dunes and flat track riders working corners like skilled craftsmen. Brown's lens seems to encompass every major AMA competition from the International Six Day Trials to ice racing to the Widowmaker Hill Climb. Dick Mann, who saws off his cast to compete at one race, is shown as both a heroic and vulnerable figure. Regular Joes with incredible talents, the racers provided an

been eclipsed by its evil twin, the outlaw biker movie. Some of the only movie footage you'll see of motorcycle racing in the 1950s and 60s appears in *The Wild One,* where Brando's Black Rebels Motorcycle Club stroll defiantly across a track, as if to offer the ultimate dis to serious competitive riding. The scene would prove very telling of the animosity that developed between motorcycle racers and outlaws during the next two decades.

Old back issues of *Cycle* magazine reveal letters from angry racers who watched the slew of biker gang movies and came away confounded and confused. *Those greasy hoodlums on those weird choppers surely didn't look like me or any of my friends,* most racers must have thought. All the while, both camps straddled an ever-widening gap in the motorcycle world. Outlaw bikers made accessible view of motorcyclists. Previously, Brown had created a similarly beatific view of surfing in *The Endless Summer* (1966), his first critically-acclaimed documentary made in the US and Australia.

Coming on the heels of the drugged-out ennui of *Easy Rider*, the real-life ugliness of Altamont—which was captured for posterity in the documentary *Gimme Shelter* (1970)—and countless biker exploitation movies, *On Any Sunday* proved such a popular respite from the norm that it received a nomination for an Academy Award for best documentary. Brown's unmitigated success did have a little to do with some of the famous company he kept: actor Steve McQueen, a life-long motorcycle enthusiast, helped produce and finance the film while starring in several segments. He appears alongside racers Malcolm Smith and Mert Lawwill, famous competitors whose presence couldn't have hurt. Best of all, Brown doesn't attempt to candy-coat motorcycle racing for mass audiences—scenes of Lawwill's racing season are full of bone-jarring crashes and shots of helmets caked with dirt from previous crack-ups. The grueling schedule that required top riders to compete in dirt track, off-road, and road racing to win the #1 AMA plate, the disheartening mechanical failures and the notorious under-funding that characterized racing three decades ago also make it into *On Any Sunday*.

Brown is famously modest about the effect *On Any Sunday* had on the public's perception of motorcycling. Still, Brown knew that his film would be vastly different from the majority of biker movies before or since. "Even today, most of the time when you see a motorcycle in a movie, it's being used to rob, pillage or do something horrible," he told *Motocross Journal* in late 1999.

For a brief while, Brown changed that perception.

With all the accolades surrounding the release of *On Any Sunday*, one of the few feature films to emerge from a major studio about motorcycle racers is almost overlooked. *Little Fauss and Big Halsy* (1970) starring Michael J. Pollard (who, by the way, appeared in *The Devil's Angels* in 1967) and Robert Redford, was an excellent character study of two very different, gypsy motorcycle racers.

Redford's Halsy and Pollard's Fauss are both determined to make their way in motorcycle racing, but go about their goals in very different ways. Handsome, confident, and ful of deceit, Halsy is a penniless, mediocre racer who envisions himself in the winner's circle via sheer guile. The baby-faced Fauss has talent on two wheels, but is a backwoods kid sorely lacking in confidence. *Little Fauss and Big Halsy* marks the return to biker movies of *Leatherboys* director Sidney J. Furie, who again spends as much time establishing the various quirks and foibles of his characters as focusing on motorcycles. Unlike his earlier motorcycle work set almost entirely at night, here, Furie works in the arid, sun-bleached American Southwest where a fine white dust seems to cover everything in sight. Fauss, who sleeps in his room with his motorcycle, is doted on by his hick parents, played brilliantly by Noah Beery and Lucille Benson. When the grinning, bullshitting Halsy shows up to take Fauss away on his first racing road trip, the movie slowly reveals the strengths and weaknesses of the two characters.

The racing scenes of off- and on-road competition are oddly disconcerting, with Furie favoring extreme close-ups and handlebar-views of the competition. The pair, who spend a summer drifting around the desert in a battered pickup truck, compete in everything from sidecar races to trials to enduros. They work hard, but seldom win anything—including each other's admiration. When their perennial loser status is combined with the film's Johnny Cash soundtrack, the hard-luck story becomes as real as a wet spark plug. While no groundbreaking piece of work, two great lead actors and a well-wrought script make *Little Fauss and Big Halsy* an entertaining and a rare look at what drives (at least some) racers to compete.

Australia's entry into the motorcycle racing feature would came in 1975, with the release of *Sidecar Racers*. This rugged, quick-paced drama stars American TV actor Ben Murphy, Aussie actress Wendy Hughes, and Peter Graves, the star of TV's *Mission Impossible*. Though the action scenes of mud-slinging, off-road racing are well-shot and exciting, the drama—and there's a lot of it—plays like a mediocre episode of TV's *Baywatch*.

Murphy plays Jeff Rayburn, a former Olympic swimming prodigy who has fallen on hard times and is convinced by a girlfriend to take up racing. Lots of shots of little open-air bike shops where Australian mechanics have rigged up some truly imaginative Honda 750 and 500-4 sidehack racers make *Sidecar Racers* at least tolerable for real enthusiasts. The bikes at work here are a weird hybrid of the skinny-tired, speedway bikes from *Once a Jolly Swagman,* though in this instance, the sidehacks are dual-purpose machines that can be run on- or off-road. As the unofficial Rodney Dangerfield of motorcycle racing, it's good to see the sidecar contingent get some film time all its own. Besides being one of the only screen acknowledgments of sidecar racing in general, *Sidecar Racers* is also notable for a scene where a bunch of Outback biker types get scared out of a motorcycle shop they're vandalizing by a girl brandishing a cricket bat! Otherwise, *Sidecar Racers,* which never caught on to establish a real following, did little to popularize the sidecar racing contingent.

Serious motorcycle racers probably cringe at the thought of stunt riders being lumped in with their lot, but the pair of dramatic re-tellings of the life of daredevil Robert "Evel" Knievel are competition films in essence. Whether it's the first film, *Evel Knievel* (1971) starring George Hamilton, or *Viva Knievel!* (1973), where the rider portrayed himself, Knievel's biggest hurdle seems to be lousy scripts.

Knievel was at his peak when the first film was made for ABC TV, and it's an entertaining enough

Vaulting a row of parked busses, bedding supermodel Lauren Hutton and starring in his own bio-pic, *Viva Knievel*, didn't prepare stunt king Evel Knievel for the greatest leap of all—from motorcycle daredevil to actor. (Warner Bros.)

chronicle of the reckless Montana kid who used sheer balls and plenty of Jack Daniels to become the world's greatest motorcycle daredevil. Unfortunately, the whole exercise reeks of sentimentality, despite Hamilton's fine acting. The better riding sequences are shot with a stunt rider looping wheelies and riding through a sorority house full of coeds on an old Triumph Tiger. These are cut with real footage from a number of Knievel's bone-smashing jumps, which are still freaky to watch 30 years later. Knievel himself is said to prefer this version of his story, which is understandable; Hamilton makes the wildman in the star-spangled leathers seem almost cuddly. The sole saving grace of *Viva Knievel!*, on the other hand, is its riding sequences. Besides that, the arcane plot involving Mexican drug smugglers who have a contract on the hero's life is the second worst career move Knievel made after the Snake River Canyon debacle.

In 1979, Britain jumped back into the motorcycle racing film genre with *Silver Dream Racer*, an action-drama starring American actor Beau Bridges as Bruce McBride and English pop star David Essex as Nick Freeman. *Silver Dream Racer* covered similar ground as *Once a Jolly Swagman* had 40 years previously, with Essex appearing as a perpetually broke amateur racer, who just happens to be long on talent. Filmed at Brands Hatch and other UK circuits, *Silver Dream Racer* is overwrought and melodramatic at times, but it's remarkably accurate in its coverage of the oversized egos of professional roadracing. The movie's treatment of race bikes is dead on as various racers supplied technical assistance to the production, including Welshman Barry Hart, who lent the film his Barton Phoenix two-stroke 50cc racer. Covered in futuristic silver bodywork, the bike was later used in an actual 1982 TT race for a third place finish. This movie also mimics *Swagman* by playing up the financial differences between privateers and factory-sponsored racers. Freeman and McBride share the affections of Julie Prince (Cristina Raines), which inevitably heightens

Rock singer-turned-grand prix racer David Essex (above) turned a respectable lap as amateur racer Nick Freeman in 1979's *Silver Dream Racer*, one of the few biker movies utilizing roadracing as a backdrop. (Almi Films)

tensions between the obnoxious American blowhard and the well-meaning British little guy. Despite the well-presented track sequences and some interesting shots of the inner workings of small race teams, *Silver Dream Racer* ends up wasting a rare chance to provide viewers with an inside view of grand prix roadracing by delving into the emotional tantrums of a soap opera.

In the nearly two decades since *Silver Dream Racer*, a slow trickle of films focused on racing motorcycles has emerged, but nothing as noteworthy as the genre's origins. Home Box Office produced *Race For Glory* (1989) another predictable—but occasionally entertaining—tale of underdog roadracers competing against arrogant

corporate interests. The movie is slightly amateurish and overly sincere, but it manages to ring true in a few spots. The difficulties in launching a race team with little money are well chronicled. And when Chris (Peter Berg) dreams out loud about building a bike with "the soul of a Harley and the power of an import" it almost seems as though we're watching the Erik Buell story.

A sequel to *On Any Sunday*, *On Any Sunday II* (1982) was produced, and this time, Don Shoemaker and Ed Forsyth handle the directing duties and they fare pretty well. However, with such a formidable first effort to compete with, there's little mystery why *On Any Sunday II* is largely considered a footnote to the first. Shoemaker and Forsyth seem too intent on recreating the innocent, unpretentious feel of the first film, even recreating the whimsical desert riding shots of the original. There are some worthwhile sequences, such as the personal interview with the calmly-cool Kenny Roberts who seems oddly mature for an untested rookie racer. Roberts is shown during his amazing winning rookie season on the world's GP circuits, a formidable level of racing he was able to master, despite enduring some anti-American prejudice from his European competitors. *On Any Sunday II* also dredges up a piece of vintage racing footage from the Elsinore Grand Prix in the early 1950s. A Yamaha enduro bike is shown, with the narrator obviously confounded by the appearance of "a motorcycle from a piano maker."

The massive technological and technique changes that would affect motorcycle racing into the 21st century are already evident in this 1986 release. Roberts, for instance, is seen exercising his unique knee-down cornering style that would revolutionize roadracing, while a lengthy segment on motocross racing featuring charismatic dirt champ Bob Hannah reveals hints of the radical suspension changes that would practically transform the sport into an airborne competition by century's end. In today's motocross world where youthful superstars like Ricky Carmichael run the show, it's great to see evidence of the early days of arenacross, where competitors like Gaylen Mosier and Marty Smith fought for simple name recognition, not million-dollar endorsement contracts.

Even greater would be a return to the racetrack by filmmakers who seem to utilize motorcycle competition for films only as a lark. There are hundreds of untold stories in racing waiting for dramatization, from the D.I.Y. career of female Harley-Davidson drag racer Angell Seeling to the late TT wonder Joey Dunlop to the inner-city rags to riches story of Team Kawasaki's drag racing champ Ricky Gadson.

Let's hope Hollywood eventually catches up.

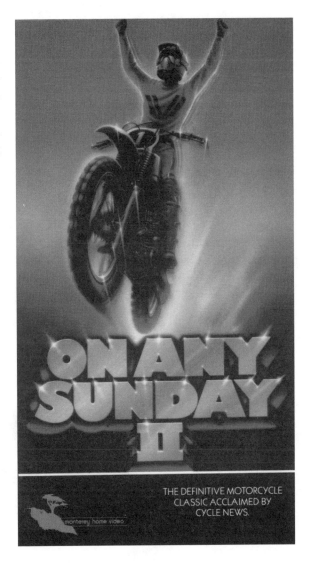

Misfits, Miscasts, and Lone Wolves

By the 1970s, filmmakers knew they couldn't continue releasing the same old biker movie again and again, because no one was going to see them. Cash register receipts made it clear that audiences were exhausted by the familiar scenes of bloodthirsty biker gangs pillaging what, by 1975, must have looked like identical versions of the same small towns. Nothing tells the story of the "Angel" genre's decline like box-office figures: *Angel Unchained* (1970) brought in a mere fraction of the income of Roger Corman's *Wild Angels,* which had earned tens of millions on the same drive-in theater circuit a mere seven years earlier when the average movie ticket cost less than half what it did in 1970.

But changing gears for producers and directors wasn't going to be easy. The country was still riding the crest of the biggest motorcycle sales boom in history in the early '70s and the appetite for two-wheeled adventure epics was still there. The problem was, (and still is) how best to transfer the visceral thrills of motorcycling to the general public without alienating—or in many instances, boring—audiences with arcane technical talk and esoteric subject matter.

For many filmmakers, the most prudent option involved simply substituting motorcycles in place of other modes of transportation. Thereby, they could produce a film easily classified and advertised as a biker movie (which was guaranteed a certain level of attendance by dedicated motorcycle enthusiasts) while using everything from urban crime dramas to medieval tales of romance for storylines. The latter provided the basis for a curious biker film, George Romero's *Knightriders* (1981). Like Camelot on two wheels, the adventure fantasy would bring movie fans who didn't know a Honda from a Husqvarna to theaters to watch what was basically a typical motorcycle club movie. Romero, who had previously made his fame, if not fortune, with the black-and-white zombie classic *Night of the Living Dead* (1968) created this oddly idyllic story. Serene and philosophical, *Knightriders* is a distinct departure from the guts and gore of his previous work. Utilizing a crew of up- and-coming actors, including Ed Harris and makeup artist-stuntman Tom Savini, Romero created a fanciful film that gently parodies the chivalry of classic medieval fables while contemporizing the underlying themes of honor

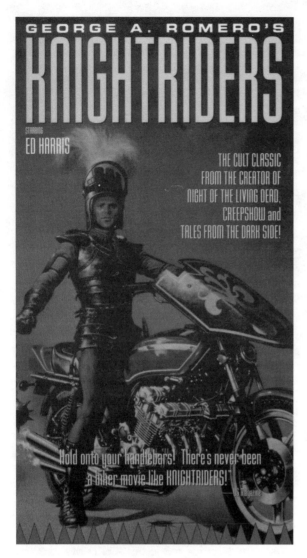

GEORGE A. ROMERO'S KNIGHTRIDERS

STARRING

ED HARRIS

THE CULT CLASSIC FROM THE CREATOR OF NIGHT OF THE LIVING DEAD, CREEPSHOW and TALES FROM THE DARK SIDE!

"Hold onto your handlebars! There's never been a biker movie like KNIGHTRIDERS!"
—US Magazine

and bravery by putting his knights on Hondas instead of horses. Harris is, for lack of a better word, "king" of a troupe of traveling renaissance fair regulars. They've carved out an interesting little world for themselves, living communally and protecting each other from mainstream society just like a motorcycle gang. The only part of the 20th Century the "Knightriders" seem interested in maintaining any sort of link with is a corral full of motorcycles. Their bikes are used mostly for competition during the group's frequent jousting exhibitions, though Harris as Billy, being regal and all, is mounted astride a gleaming red Honda CBX. The mechanical complexity and sheer heft of the six-cylinder superbike is a clever visual device, as the diminutive Harris looks fittingly noble while riding.

And while it often appears that *Knightriders* will get bogged down in a script leaden with grandiose appeals to common decency and chivalry, the film breaks free by presenting some truly inspired motorcycle stunt work. During the jousting sequences, Romero's stunt coordinators rigged several of the dirt bikes to sever on impact, which is simply spectacular when viewed, even on a small screen. Others tumble headlong with their riders vaulting dramatically skyward—just try that on a horse. Romero also manages to provide some genuinely entertaining moments as the troupe find themselves harassed by backwoods cops (again, just as biker gangs had) and encountering problems with in-fighting and professional jealousies. And just like movie biker gangs, the Knightriders face the constant hassle of insufficient funds. The scenes where the Knightriders are ostracized by insensitive locals should be familiar to anyone who's ever watched a biker movie. Re-launching them under the premise of a medieval fantasy flick was a crafty mix of metaphors from Romero.

The camaraderie shared by the Knightriders was actually fostered on the movie's set, said longtime Romero crew member Nick "Bomba" Tallo. During the daily ride from the film's offices to production sites in the Pennsylvania backwoods, Tallo said the movie's stunt riders routinely passed by a motorcycle dealership. Approaching the shop, the Knightriders crew would pull long wheelies past the shop, which, on occasion, prompted competing stunts from local riders who sometimes gathered to watch the film crew pass by. *Knightriders* didn't exactly set any attendance records, but it has developed a cult following among some bikers. It has proven most popular with medieval history buffs and renaissance fair re-enactors who've lionized the cast's devotion to anachronism and chivalry.

With *Knightriders,* Romero showed other directors that all biker movies didn't have to be the same. Then again, that point had been well stated by director James Guerico with *Electra Glide in Blue* (1973). Motorcycle cops hadn't been featured in a full-length dramatic film since stuntman-turned-actor Ralph Meeker carried the lead in the classic *Code Two* (1953). Meeker's Harley-mounted highway patrolmen ride undercover

One of the better character studies of motorcyclists on film, *Electra Glide in Blue* (1973) presented the moral ambiguities endured by an ambitious young highway patrolman played by Robert Blake (at right). (United Artists)

against an interstate ring of truck hijackers, and reveal for the first time on film how effective motorcycles could be in law enforcement. *Code Two's* dated, but altogether entertaining script is typical 1950s cop fare, with actor and motorcycle enthusiast Keenan Wynn turning in a typically salty performance as Meeker's partner. Lengthy road riding sequences are as good as they get, with director Fred Wilcox's use of trailer-mounted cameras providing an excellent on-bike perspective.

But where *Code Two* only glossed over the motivations, insecurities, and personal demons of the average motorcycle cop, *Electra Glide in Blue* takes us deep into the head of Robert Blake's Sgt. John Wintergreen, where we experience the world through his eyes, warts and all. This intense study of a man consumed by his physical limitations (he's only 5'5") and unbridled ambition (he wants to make lieutenant) is one of the

decade's better film characterizations. *Electra Glide in Blue,* which was a bigger hit in Europe than in the US, helped make a legitimate star out of the scrappy Blake, who went on to star in TV's *Baretta.* The role was custom made for Blake who had frequently fought for roles written for taller actors. An avid motorcyclist, Blake, who got his start in the *Our Gang* children's comedy shorts, had ridden a bike in Truman Capote's *In Cold Blood* back in 1967. *Electra Glide,* named for the massive V-Twin bikes that the Harley-Davidson Motor Company produced specifically for touring and police department use, presents the polar opposite side of the biker story. It lends insight into motorcycle cops who were too often depicted only writing tickets and generally harassing movie bikers.

Artfully photographed with an eye for extreme close-ups and detail, Guerico's film takes the

A JAMES WILLIAM GUERCIO-RUPERT HITZIG
Production

MGM/UA
HOME VIDEO

the other square cops by, you can almost feel his confusion.

Filmed entirely in the deserts of New Mexico and Arizona, *Electra Glide in Blue* follows a murder mystery involving an incoherent hermit—played deftly by Elisha Cook—and a large sum of money. The complex plot makes it one of the few biker movies to be regularly included in discussions of "serious" films of the 1970s, and a frequent favorite on house revival schedules. And this praise comes despite some grisly violence and a few standard chase scenes. But what will likely stick with viewers is the surprise ending which plays almost like a negative of the finale of *Easy Rider.* In this instance, the long-hairs are the villains, a statement that was both shocking and original when it hit the screen during the psychedelic seventies.

The always interesting relationship between cops and bikers also caught the imagination of George Miller, a young Australian director with one of the best cinematic eyes for chaos ever. For *Mad Max* (1979), Miller took an unknown, aspiring actor named Mel Gibson, clad him in skintight black leather and re-named him Max. Max is a cop from the near future who faces down marauding gangs of bikers possessed of a uniquely Australian brand of ugliness. Max lives in an Outback Aussie hamlet so idyllic that even the ominous shadow of a vaguely-explained societal breakdown can't taint its panoramic beauty. Miller makes it clear that Max has it all: he waves goodbye every morning to a beautiful wife and their new baby and enjoys the camaraderie of his fellow officers. One thing he doesn't have is his own voice.

The film's distributors didn't entrust Max or any other characters to use their own voices, assuming the heavy Australian accents would alienate American audiences. The choice to dub Americanized English over the final cut nearly corrupts *Mad Max* with a B-movie cheapness it doesn't deserve. Thankfully, this wrongheaded decision doesn't detract from the wild action sequences that made it a favorite at drive-in theaters from Brisbane to Buffalo. The biker gang members in this movie are a peculiar, loose-knit bunch, covered in an assortment of furs and pieced-together costumes that would be more at

physical vastness and bigger-than-life personalities of the American Southwest and distorts them with the deftness of Robert Altman. Wintergreen is forced to contend with faded beauty queens and petulant hippies, sadistic superior officers and pig-ignorant locals. Worst of all, Wintergreen hates his job as a motorcycle cop, referring to his bike as "that elephant under my ass." Even the relationship between the brooding, agnostic Wintergreen and his dopey, bellicose partner The Zipper, verges on strangeness. The pair alternately grate on each other's nerves, philosophize about life, and lazily peruse Wonder Woman comic books during slow moments on their shifts. By the movie's end, Wintergreen is so unsure of whether his side is right in its crusade against a society that seems to have passed him and all of home on the set of *Conan the Barbarian*. Riding European-style café racers and wearing full face helmets, the gang provided American audiences with one of their first glances of the blossoming performance bike cult that was gaining momentum worldwide. Instead of being content just blasting along the Outback roads at triple-digit speeds, this gang inevitably takes their high-speed game of cat and mouse with the highway patrol too far. They torch The Goose, one of Max's police pals after his upended cruiser leaks gasoline. Max, horrified at the mutilation of his friend, begins what will become a three-movie descent into emotional burnout.

The remainder of *Mad Max* is one long, frantic, almost surreal chase sequence, with each crash (one of which actually resulted in the death of a stuntman during filming) and roadside showdown more sadistic than the last. In many scenes, Max's supercharged Ford Mustang and the various Kawasaki and Suzuki superbikes were run so fast it looks as if the film speed had been altered—according to Miller, it hadn't. And when Max has his left leg nearly severed by a speeding bike, the injury ends up playing well in the subsequent sequels to galvanize Max's *hardened survivor* image. All of this high-speed, high-octane road carnage was timed just right for movie audiences expecting more and bigger thrills for their biker movie dollar. In seconds, a single shot of a bike hurtling into an 18-wheeler at 140 mph made the chain-whippings and barroom brawls of *Bury Me An Angel* seem absolutely tame by comparison. It also made Miller realize what a winning formula he had with his embittered, rogue Aussie cop. Production was begun in 1983 on *The Road Warrior* (or Mad Max II), proving *Mad Max* to be one of the only biker movies popular enough to earn a sequel, and a superior sequel at that.

From the lengthy opening montage and voice-over, it becomes readily apparent that whatever societal ills had plagued the Australia of *Mad Max*, they'd really gone to pot for *The Road Warrior*. A Third World War over dwindling oil resources, a narrator tells us, prompted a full-bore slide into world anarchy, and, as we soon learn, an unchecked outbreak of punk-rock fashion designers. Everywhere viewers look in *The Road Warrior* there are studded dog collars, football

shoulder pads, shredded leather bodysuits, and enough multi-colored hair dye to equip a Sex Pistols reunion. Audiences loved it, despite the homoerotic overtones of an all-male biker gang run by a naked bodybuilder in a hockey goalie's mask. The story opens with an excellent bike-car chase scene, and to the delight of action movie fans everywhere, ends with the same. In a future where oil conglomerates had been wiped out by war, gasoline had become the world's most precious resource. Entire societies had ceased to function when the pumps ran dry of what our narrator calls "the black fuel" and, coming just seven years after the US fuel crisis, it was a broad indictment of our dependence on fossil fuels. This premise helped to make *The Road Warrior* an

CITY LIMITS
THE LINES ARE DRAWN.
FIGHT FOR YOUR FUTURE.

DARRELL LARSON   JOHN STOCKWELL   RAE DAWN CHONG
ROBBY BENSON   KIM CATTRALL   JAMES EARL JONES

Mainly, an even more sinister gang of bikers than those Gibson faced in *Mad Max.* These bikers are intent on pirating the final remaining tanker of gas for their own hedonistic ends and will stop at nothing to get it.

"On the roads it was a white-line nightmare. Only those mobile enough to scavenge and brutal enough to pillage could survive" comes a portentous voice-over from the narrator, and he couldn't have been more right. In 1982, the humor magazine National Lampoon commented that the most dangerous place in America on a Saturday night wasn't a street corner in South Central Los Angeles, but "the parking lot of a redneck drive-in after a showing of *The Road Warrior.*" The motorcycles Miller used in his second film were, again, Kawasaki Z-1s, Honda Supersports, and a few dirt bikes of various makes, but they've been so heavily disguised with futuristic bodywork and makeshift weaponry, the big Kaws and Hondas are identifiable only by their meaty, four-cylinder howl. Despite the movie's setting along the remote, arid highways of the Australian Outback, motorcycles do not play a prominent role in *The Road Warrior.* Instead, a whole squadron of mechanical hybrid machines are thrown into battle by the biker army, some comprising bits from what appear to be dune buggies and abandoned cars, while others are elaborately altered dirt bikes sporting flame-throwers and machine-gun emplacements.

Filling theater seats and drive-in spaces like few biker movies had in over a decade, the twin *Mad Max* films quickly spawned a whole catalog of post-apocalyptic action movies.

Among them was *City Limits* (1985). For a B-movie, it had a surprisingly talented cast, including James Earl Jones, Rae Dawn Chong, and Kim Cattrall. With the usual nuclear wars, plagues, and diseases having wiped out much of civilization, the only things left on earth seem to be warring biker gangs (in this instance the Clippers and the DA's) and streets that bear a disturbing resemblance to modern-day Detroit. When an evil multinational corporation moves in to rebuild the ruined city, they enlist the DA's to help them. This results in some colorful, bike-to-bike battles and lots of thinly-veiled warnings about common people being exploited by corporate greed.

unlikely message movie; an ecological parable cleverly disguised as an action flick.

That's about the only real-life parallel evident here. Unlike the early biker movies, the spate of post-apocalyptic biker movies were pure fantasy. As a result, they drew audiences who typically preferred science fiction and horror to motorcycle movies while no longer affecting the public's perception of everyday motorcyclists. However farfetched, *The Road Warrior* is engaging as it chronicles the plight of a small desert compound occupied by a collection of saintly survivors. They take in the grizzled loner Max on the condition that he pilot an ancient 18-wheeler to a fabled promised land where, apparently, gas stations, or the ability to live without them, still exists. There's a catch in reaching the promised land.

The whole end-of-the-world biker movie scenario didn't actually originate with *Mad Max* as is commonly believed. It was Roger Corman, director of so many American International Pictures' 1960s biker movies who first merged futuristic-post-nuclear wastelands and motorcycles in *Deathsport* (1978). In this release, David "Kung Fu" Carradine is Kaz Oshay, a "Ranger Guide" which is something akin to a nomad Samurai warrior. Dressed in a mixture of furs and silly-looking capes, Carradine and his shapely co-star, former Playboy Bunny Claudia Jennings, end up, by various twists of fate, defending themselves against cannibals, mutants, and dirt-bike riding townspeople. Regardless of the foe, all the fight scenes seem specifically designed to show off Jenning's curves. As the sequel to the cult classic *Death Race 2000*, *Deathsport* has none of the earlier film's bizarre black humor, nor does it contain the fast-motion, road-rage thrills. Instead, Corman fills his movie with all sorts of cheesy special effects, including a disappearance device that looks suspiciously like a can of Maxwell House, over-wrought explosions, and dirt bikes (or "death machines" in this instance) that are so covered in fairings and "futuristic" technology, they're barely rideable.

With a legion of imitators hot on his heels, Miller directed one more segment in the *Mad Max* trilogy, but the overblown dramatics of *Mad Max: Beyond Thunderdome* (1984) reveals that the director might have fared better had he stopped while he was ahead. Starring singer Tina Turner as the sovereign of "Bartertown," a city of absolute wretchedness carved out of the desert, *Thunderdome* has little of the manic action and even less of the multi-vehicle carnage that made the first two movies so memorable. Still, it was a better effort than some of the imitators, many of which were as frightful as the nuclear holocausts they implied. Budgets for films like *Billy Badd* (1993), could be alarmingly low as all filmmakers needed to simulate a wasteland was a desert and a few weather-beaten leather jackets. With little more than a borrowed premise—the movie opens with a rolling shot of a yellow highway line and an ominous, echo-leaden voice-over just like *The Road Warrior*—*Billy Badd* reveals how influential the George Miller-Mel Gibson collaborations

ROGER CORMAN CLASSICS

DIGITALLY REMASTERED

DAVID CARRADINE IN

DEATHSPORT

DEATH SPORT ISN'T JUST A GAME. IN THE YEAR 3000, IT'S THE ONLY WAY TO SURVIVE!

Includes Leonard Maltin's exclusive interview with Roger Corman.

were. We know we're in for a bad time when, during the opening credits, a woman's voice declares, "we believed that all things good would come to those who drove East, to New York City." She'd obviously never met Mayor Giuliani. Nevertheless, the main characters Frankie and Zoey (with no apologies to J.D. Salinger) soon encounter Billy Badd, a sadistic motorcyclist who favors pounding his mohawked head and whooping war cries into the wind. Billy targets the couple's vintage VW bus and proceeds to make their lives hell, nearly as much of a hell as that of any viewer stuck watching this movie draw to its psychotic and entirely predictable close.

When considering oddball biker movie formulas, perhaps none were weirder and more

GOD FORGIVES...
THE BLACK ANGELS
DON'T

BLACK ANGELS

DES ROBERTS • LINDA JACKSON • JOHN KING III
Co-starring CLANCY SYRKO • BEVERLY GARDNER • JAMES WHITWORTH

gangs. Huggy Bear meets Sonny Barger, and the results are as bad as movie making gets. Filled with the same stilted, "jive turkey" dialogue and cheesy disco music of black exploitation films like *Cleopatra Jones* and Rudy Rae Moore's *Avenging Disco Godfather*, *The Black Six* is one of the few movies ever made that manages to offend all races equally with its tired stereotyping.

As a sign of how weird the times were, the National Football League actually sanctioned six of its biggest celebrities to star in this exercise in hokum. The opening credits even list the team affiliations of Miami Dolphin Mercury Morris, Pittsburgh Steeler "Mean" Joe Greene, San Francisco 49er Gene Washington, Minnesota Viking Carl Eller, Cincinnati Bengal Lem Barney, and Willie Lanier. Eller, who went on to become a Minnesota Supreme Court Justice, here bears a disturbing likeness to actor Samuel L. Jackson. Of the half-dozen main characters, only Mercury Morris seems to take to acting as well as the All-Pro running back did the gridiron. His flip personality and quick way with a joke makes *The Black Six* nearly watchable. There's even a cameo by Oakland Raider's defensive end Ben Davidson who plays Thor, a stoned gang leader in a horned Viking helmet. Davidson delivers his lines as if he's portraying a biblical figure in *The Ten Commandments*.

The racial conflict at the core of this film centers around Bubba Daniel's (Gene Washington's) younger brother Eddie, a high school football star who has the grand misfortune to date a white girl whose brother, Moose, is the leader of a racist motorcycle gang. In a scene shot at night with few lights and even fewer microphones, Moose, replete with a Harry Reems mustache and a chopped Hog, chases Eddie around the football field, chain whipping him to death in a feeble fight scene that's too silly to be startling or believable. To the rescue come the sextet of football stars who are portraying a group of recently returned Vietnam veterans. They tell an old woman who takes them in from the road and feeds them, "We go anywhere the wind takes us. There ain't no

offensive than movies like *Black Angels* (1971) and *The Black Six* (1974). These two turkeys managed to insult minorities, bikers, and the entire Civil Rights movement in less than three hours combined. The makers of both films saw potential to add to the terror of invading cycle gangs the specter of forced integration. In the end, adding racial conflict to the usual tale of battling biker gangs did little to electrify a tired premise other than to provide some goofy dialogue and awkward posturing about "black power, baby." *The Black Angels* was one of the few screen acknowledgments of the sometimes tense relations between white and black outlaw motorcycle gangs, but it made a savage free-for-all out of what, in reality, was a shared coexistence. This effort, if you can call it that, was followed by *The Black Six*, a cheapo classic that attempts to juxtapose the emerging black consciousness movement with the world of biker

> "I'm gonna kill you, you no good egg-suckin', finger-lickin', snot-pickin', scuzzy faced rat."
> *The Black Angels*

Jamie Rose (left), and Catherine Carlen (right), ride hard and kill plenty of zombies as members of the Cycle Sluts, an all-female gang featured in the 1989 sci-fi comedy *Chopper Chicks in Zombie Town*. **(Troma Team/New Line Video)**

tomorrow, just right now." In 1991, *Chrome Soldiers* would completely borrow this premise to put Gary Busey and a crew of middle-aged bikers together to right similar wrongs in an identical small town.

The Black Six all ride bone stock Triumph Bonnevilles and three-cylinder Tridents, which makes for some funny scenes in which, for some reason, the sound technicians dub in the wail of two-stroke dirt bikes when the gang rides in formation. Minutes later, the burble of the Triumph's horizontal two and three cylinder motors are disguised with the roar of unmuffled Harleys, which the filmmakers must have figured would be more thrilling for viewers. It only takes ten minutes of film for the brothers to encounter their first of many racist rednecks, who, for some reason, are crazy enough to start fights with a group of guys who look like refugees from Muscle Beach. Even

> "You women are Sluts, try and act like it!"
> Rox (Catherine Carlen)
> to her female gang
> *Chopper Chicks in Zombietown*

more ridiculous is a scene where the gang is forced to defend itself by tearing apart a small country tavern. Morris saunters in amongst the cowboy hats and rebel flags and annoys the other customers by playing loud soul music on the jukebox: only in Hollywood do redneck watering holes keep Marvin Gaye records on their jukeboxes.

After Washington's sister—who sports an afro bigger than the entire Jackson 5 combined—lectures the gang on their lack of ethnic responsibility, they decide to avenge the dead little brother, even if it means taking on two whole gangs of outlaw bikers. Like nearly all black exploitation movies (and biker movies for that matter) *The Black Six* is part detective drama, part action movie and heavy on social posturing. Director William Swenning also filled his first feature effort with enough overacting to fuel an entire

season of dinner theater. *The Black Six* has all the production value of an amateur porno flick, so it's not a surprise to find within its 91 minutes two of the worst fight scenes in all biker filmdom. With reality fully suspended, the climactic battle finds the Black Six surrounded by about 100 enemies, who, in classic martial arts movie style, choose to attack one or two at a time. If increased consciousness of racial strife was the aim then it failed at this goal more miserably than did the Los Angeles riots. Adding insult to injury, the movie's end credits carry a dismal quote from the theme song, warning, "Honky watch out, hassle a brother and the Black Six might return." Thankfully for movie audiences and bikers everywhere, that never happened.

If this seems bad, consider the portrayals of women in biker movies. From the earliest days, producers have latched on to the idea of switching gender in biker movies to draw in audiences hoping to see a few cat fights. *Mini Skirt Mob* (1968) and *Hell's Belles* (1969) both attempted to reveal that lady bikers could be just as savage and sexual as their male counterparts. But it took Roger Corman's lesser-known brother Gene to concoct *Darktown Strutters* (1975) a movie that somehow managed to capture both the sexism of female biker movies and the urban hokum of the black exploitation genre. In this disco-mystery-biker flick, a quartet of soul-singing, black women bikers is hunting down a team of dirt-biking racists who have kidnapped one of their own—and apparently the script writer as well. Thankfully, these portrayals, unlike those of the various "Angel" films of the 1960s, were hardly the sort of movies that could offend bikers. The characterizations were so over-the-top, there were few people who could believe the hard-as-nails lady riders in *Chopper Chicks in Zombie Town* (1989) had anything to do with real bikers.

A more realistic and gritty portrayal of urban biker life emerged from The Netherlands and director Paul Verhoeven with *Spetters* (1980). Set among a group of youthful motorcycle enthusiasts near Amsterdam, *Spetters* is an unflinching look at a group of European riders but, because of its strong sexuality, never made it to American release. Verhoeven, who later directed *Robocop* and *Basic Instinct*, was already revealing his penchant for the seamier, tougher side of life as he pit Rutger Hauer as a champion motocross racer against a motley assortment of young would-be racers determined to achieve similar success. In the process of attempting to usurp the champ, two racers, Hans, Reen and Fientja, a small-town girl determined to sleep her way to the top, all get their comeuppance, ending up either crippled or destroyed by broken dreams. Verhoeven pulls no punches in dramatizing the competitiveness of amateur racing, including the hard living and blind ambition that consumes his characters. Uncensored versions of *Spetters* contain some gnarly brawls and ugly gang-rape scenes, which, in the finest European tradition, are fully X-rated. *Spetters* is not for everyone, but some critics have described the complex plot as full of minute details that can keep viewers interested—or at least shaking their heads in disbelief—for several screenings.

Another attempt to transcend the boundaries of biker movies came from action movie director Walter Hill with *Streets of Fire* (1984). Hill, who was responsible for making comedian Eddie Murphy a star with *48 Hours* in 1982, altered the *biker gang invades small town* theme in both time and aesthetic in *Streets of Fire,* subtitled "A Rock and Roll Fable." It's more like a two-hour music video. But like even the most self-indulgent music videos, *Streets of Fire* is often visually engaging. It's even more enjoyable if viewers don't take the corny plot lines too seriously. Calling this movie's dialogue stiff would be like accusing Kaw-Li-Ga, the cigar store Indian, of wooden acting; it's a given. But with its stagy, choreographed violence, rich visuals, and a rollicking soundtrack by slide guitar master Ry Cooder and L.A. rockabilly outfit The Blasters, *Streets of Fire* is at least an enjoyable departure from the norm.

Shot on a soundstage by cinematographer Andrew Laszlo, *Streets of Fire* is set in a town so dingy and frayed it makes present day Youngstown look inviting. The storyline follows the kidnapping of rock singer Ellen Aim, a hometown-girl made-good played with a series of snarls and squeals by Diane Lane. Her kidnapper is a particularly pasty-faced Willem Dafoe. Dafoe leads the Bombers, a greaser biker gang who look like they've raided the Stray Cats' dressing room for costumes. It's seldom daylight in the netherworld where *Streets of Fire* is set, and the rain and fog are so thick they part dramatically around the wheels of the antique hot rods everybody drives. Even the Bomber's motorcycles are designed to suit the gloomy mood. The entire phalanx of low-slung Harley lowriders and old choppers are painted flat black, including the gas tanks and even the chromework.

Our hero Tom Cody is played by Michael Pare from *Eddie and the Cruisers.* With a permanent smirk, Pare plays his reluctant rescuer role for every ounce of Humphrey Bogart he can muster. Some of Pare's lines are so absurdly macho the whole movie takes on an air of farce. Comedian Rick Moranis is also a scream as a cynical concert

promoter characterized by a big mouth and an even bigger wad of cash. Watch for a young Bill Paxton who makes an appearance as a nerdy, gap-toothed bartender. With such lampooned characters, it's never made clear whether Hill intended it as a serious thriller, a campy take-off on biker movies, juvenile delinquent films, or action movies in general.

Take Cody, for instance. As a surprise to no one, we find that he once dated the kidnapped rock star. Jilted but faithful, he becomes so driven to rescue Lane that he and his butch sidekick McCoy—played androgynously by Amy Madigan—take on the Bombers, all 200 of them, and in the gang's headquarters, no less. Armed with a "custom-made" rifle that miraculously shoots straight even after being used to club a dozen bikers, Pare

Perry King   Sylvester Stallone   Henry Winkler

The Lords of Flatbush

"A small masterpiece..."
— Time Out

Hill's nostalgic look at greaser-era biking had actually been one-upped a dozen years earlier by *The Lords of Flatbush* (1974) an excellent, ensemble cast picture with Henry Winkler, Perry King, and Sylvester Stallone. A coming-of-age tale set in an Italian neighborhood in 1950s Brooklyn, *Lords* presents the chummy lifestyle of four young friends whose rebelliousness is cut short by the unexpected onset of adulthood. The Lords are a small group, too mischievous and dopey to actually be labeled a gang, and their lack of venom made this movie well-liked by a wide variety of viewers. King, an actor who is an avid rider in his off-stage time, pilots a vintage Harley-Davidson Panhead Duo Glide, while the others make do by standing around on street corners incessantly clowning and combing their pompadours.

Neither *Streets of Fire* nor *The Lords of Flatbush* came close to the moody, film noir cult classic, *The Loveless* (1982). This was a movie, like *Electra Glide in Blue,* that proved a bigger hit with the art house set than the general biking public. The slow-moving, highly stylized feature was the brainchild of revisionist rock singer Robert Gordon, who appears as former death row convict Davis. Gordon is an entertainer whose uniquely Eisenhower-era view of the world came startlingly to life in his first starring role. Critics have heaped praise on *The Loveless* calling the film "stunning; an Edward Hopper painting of life in the 50s" and "a look at life during postwar America few people have seen."

Director Kathryn Bigelow's camera work is some of the most memorable and stirring to be found in any biker movie. Unhurried shots take in every nuance and architectural detail of vintage roadside diners, from the blue tattoos on a customer's hand, to the flies gathering along a neon Coca-Cola sign. One scene, where Willem Dafoe's Vance orders a plate of bacon and eggs, is filmed in actual time, with five minutes clicking slowly, listlessly, by while he combs his pompadour and waits for his breakfast. If all of this sounds a bit pretentious, well, it was. But after dozens of films made with few artistic allusions, *The Loveless* revealed an underlying visual richness to the motorcycle subculture.

Bathed in vintage rock music, the film actually does have something of a plot at work, but you'll

is the ultimate *ubermensch*, a Lone Ranger who's so over-the-top, Tonto wouldn't recognize him. Hill is obviously mining from or making homage to 1950s camp-musicals like *The Girl Can't Help It*, thinly-scripted films intended to further the careers of up-and-coming rock stars. Though there are no rock stars in *Streets of Fire*, Hill breaks up the fights and fury every few minutes with a musical number, creating a movie that feels like Rogers and Hammerstein's *Oklahoma* with switchblades. *Streets of Fire* ends predictably after Pare defeats Dafoe in a street fight—using sledgehammers, no less—that's long even by movie standards. Regardless of the director's intentions, *Streets of Fire* is a pleasant enough send-up of biker movies and captures some of the look and feel of 1950s B-movies in general.

have to unhinge your hypnotic gaze from the antique motorcycles and frequent views of the Georgia countryside to catch it. On their way to the races in Daytona, Davis, Vance, and a trio of other bikers are forced to make a repair stop in a burg so small Dafoe asks a waitress "is this a town or a truck stop?" Vance soon finds himself in a tryst with the teenage daughter of the village bully. Tarver (J. Don Ferguson) also happens to hold considerable clout amongst the town's dozen or so inhabitants and, if the bikers can stop smoking Lucky Strikes or admiring their reflections long enough, they might notice themselves to be in a spot of trouble from an over-protective Dad.

Predictable results ensue, but any action in this movie definitely takes a back seat to the director's eye for the artistic. And the script that Bigelow co-wrote with Monty Montgomery contains one of the coolest biker movie lines since Brando's Johnny was asked what he was rebelling against: after a waitress tells Dafoe that her husband committed suicide, she then asks Dafoe what he thinks about the town.

"I think your husband had the right idea," he shoots back.

If Walter Hill and Kathryn Bigelow were content to look at biker movies through a nostalgic lens, director David Kellogg was looking toward the future for answers when

Retro rockabilly singer Robert Gordon strikes a classic rebel pose while starring in the 1982 biker art film *The Loveless*. This slow-paced period drama even featured a soundtrack of Gordon's Elvis-inspired music. (Pioneer Films)

he created *Cool As Ice* (1991), a star vehicle for the erstwhile Pat Boone of rap music, Vanilla Ice. With its emphasis on the growing trend of urban sportbike and hip-hop cultures, Kellogg's viewfinder was undoubtedly pointed in the right direction. But somehow the script, like Vanilla Ice's raps themselves, wears thin after a very few minutes. This leaves viewers to suffer through a two-hour performance by a young man so full of himself he doesn't even wince when reciting lines like "get rid of the zero, and get with the hero."

Where *Cool as Ice* fails most is in its mission to represent the sportbike culture, because a film about sportbikes and the people who ride them is long overdue. The death-defying canyon racing scene in California has become motorcycling legend and the new generation of race-replica bikes

have made the bearded outlaw on his Harley chopper about as relevant to today's Kawasaki Ninja-riding youths as a Roaring Twenties flapper doing the Charleston. Instead of exploring what motivates youthful motorcyclists to ride at 160 mph on public streets, *Cool As Ice* simply props up flimsy adversaries and reluctant girlfriends for Vanilla Ice, a/k/a Rob Van Winkle, to push over or win over. The film actually follows a similar plot as *The Loveless*. Ice, playing a rapper named Johnny Van Owen, suffers mechanical failure on his lime green Kawasaki Ninja 750 on the way home from a concert. And, for the first time in recorded history, said rap concert just happens to have taken place near a small, nameless country town. There's nothing for Johnny and his posse to do but kick back and pause for

Hoping to extend the career of rapper and real-life biker Vanilla Ice (a/k/a Rob Van Winkle), Universal City Studios created *Cool As Ice* in 1991, a modern take on the bad-boy-biker-meets-small-town-girl saga. (Universal City Studios)

several days in order to make repairs. Quite naturally, the girl Ice chooses to woo has a father who "objects to that young man's appearance," but what's to dislike about Johnny, who runs about in a size XXX jacket and jeans, both covered in more slogans and corporate logos than a NASCAR trailer?

Cool As Ice has been dismissed by rap fans and biker movie aficionados alike, though there's never a shortage of good-humored types willing to rent the video for a few late night beer-party laughs. More than anything, *Cool As Ice* accomplished two things: in the gangsta rap era, it made urban music and its followers seem more pathetic than threatening, and it also alerted the world to just how desperately it needs a serious, or at least entertaining, film about street racers.

We almost got one, albeit an animated version, with *Akira* (1988). In the best tradition of Japanese science-fiction, this feature-length epic is set in "neo-Tokyo" after a nuclear holocaust. With fluid, crisp animation, and the angular, dense illustrations typical of Japanese pulp comics, *Akira* begins with an intriguing tale about a group of teenage bikers who inhabit a seedy, neon-lit section of Tokyo. Akira, Kineda, Tetsuo, and friends spend their nights popping pills and riding a collection of futuristic race bikes, which are obviously derived from the hypersports machines popular in 1990s Japan and Europe. But these bikes, which are covered in plastic bodywork and corporate sponsorship logos, feature "ceramic double-coated two-wheel drive" and "computer controlled anti-lock brakes." Telling of the rapid climb of superbike technology in the late 1990s, the single-sided swingarms and anti-lock brakes would become commonplace on real Japanese bikes a few years later.

Akira's gang members are reminiscent of the aimless Droogs from the film adaptation of Anthony Burgess' *A Clockwork Orange,* as they seem to rumble with other gangs almost out of a lack of anything better to do. Their chief rivals are the Clowns, a bizarre bunch on choppers who dress like members of a circus troupe outfitted by the Hell's Angels. But the gang fights and barroom brawls that occupy most of the gang's time are nothing compared to the cataclysms that envelop—and eventually destroy—neo Tokyo when the nervous, edgy Akira starts to develop mutant superpowers. *Akira* is an epic, which means there are many conflicting and recurring sub plots. Pay close attention, or you will come away with nothing more than an eyeful of dazzling visuals. At times, the streets are clogged by massive student protests as society comes crashing down in the face of nuclear Armageddon. This, however, does little to deter Akira's buddies from pursuing the quickly-mutating teenager throughout town, attacking him with lasers, bazookas, and motorcycles capable of flying over buildings when necessary.

As Akira's telekinetic powers multiply, he grows larger than Godzilla, frequently suffering brain-seizures that level entire blocks of buildings. The ending, which many viewers found famously muddy, is tough to understand because *Akira* was derived from a 40-issue comic book serial. Reportedly, the comic book's authors didn't want the film to reveal the yet-unpublished series finale, so an alternate and very abrupt finish was written for the film, leaving a more satisfying finish for comic book fans only. Regardless of the ending, there's blood and gore to spare here, and the film's kinetic, frantic animation is a visual feast. The animators present so many small details and wild scenes that the best way to watch it is on a big screen. Then again, when viewed on video, important scenes can be watched dozens of times. From the architectural over-development of modern-day Tokyo to the peculiar Japanese biker gang custom of dragging a samurai sword along the pavement to create a shower of sparks, *Akira's* creator, Katsuhiro Otomo, creates a compelling and occasionally disturbing vision of biking in the future.

If *Akira* delivered a charred, horrifying look at biking's future, *Roadside Prophets* (1991) delivered its future sunny-side up. A truly odd piece of new wave filmmaking, *Roadside Prophets* is a desert adventure flick starring cowpunk singer John Doe as Joe. Joe is a cynical Harley rider who has promised to bury the ashes of a former friend at a Las Vegas casino. The only catch is that Joe never received specific instructions on how to find the casino. Out on the highway, Joe runs into an increasingly weird and quirky cast of characters, including David "Kung Fu" Carradine as a genuine roadside prophet who sits by the highway spewing nonsensical philosophy, and folk singer Arlo Guthrie as a groovy bartender. Joe, who hates his job, his life, his ex-wife, and everything except his beloved '59 Harley Panhead, is ripe for a spiritual journey, even if he winds up having a jerky punk kid, Sam (played by Beastie Boy Adam Horowitz) along for the ride. Like *Easy Rider* run through the lens of *Repo Man, Roadside Prophets* is anything but representative of a generation: instead of looking for answers, it just ambles along slowly, going nowhere. Horowitz's impressionable young character, Sam, knows nothing about bikes and comes along because he couldn't get up the courage to commit suicide by jumping off his apartment roof. Joe, on the other hand, in his always languid tone, seems to move through the heatwaved landscape like smoke, alternately annoyed by, and pitying his partner.

Where the rednecks in *Easy Rider* offered the bikers a taste of 12-gauge buckshot, the farmer who stops to assist this pair is played by LSD guru Timothy Leary. Leary offers transcendental insights while John Cusack appears as Casper, a crazed, one-eyed diner patron who eats an entire menu's fare in one sitting. There's so many zany characters, *Roadside Prophets* seems more intent on shocking viewers than on relating a story. Nevertheless, this exercise in strangeness-for-strangeness-sake is an entertaining change from the usual biker movie fare, even if *Roadside Prophets* leaves most viewers scratching their heads in bewilderment long after the movie has ended.

These oddball biker movies may not have set the critics alight with praise, or reached any new attendance records. But their jocular, offbeat characterizations were a pleasant and wholly entertaining break from the sinister view of bikers that had caused so much ill will with the public.

The Anti-Hero
Becomes a Hero

By the middle of the 1980s, the public's perception of bikers had changed drastically from that of only ten or twenty years before. Some blame a gradual graying of the Wild Ones from the 1960s, whose lifestyles began to reflect the mellowing of age. Over the next two decades biker gangs would continue to make headlines in the international press for everything from links to organized crime to massive illegal drug operations, but the average Joe chain-wallet Harley rider was a markedly different breed of biker than his long-haired, one-percenter predecessor.

Gone were the barroom brawls and group sex of the 1960s, replaced by biker-sponsored charitable events like Harley-Davidson's annual Muscular Dystrophy campaign which, by the mid-1980s, was raising millions to fight disease each year. With many of the motorcycle gang members jailed or disbanded, most news coverage of outlaw bikers was limited to shots of long columns of bearded Hog riders delivering Christmas toys for needy kids at Toys for Tots rallies. This conscious alteration of the biker persona from plunderer to philanthropist could trace its roots back to the peak of the 60s outlaw era. That's when some

clubs began carrying elaborately embossed business cards which members would distribute to stranded motorists after offering them freelance roadside assistance. *"You have just been assisted by a member of the Devil's Disciples motorcycle club. When we do right, no one remembers. When we do wrong, no one lets us forget."* was a typical message. However noble their intentions, the sight of a pack of grungy outlaws pulling over en masse to help grandma's Dodge Dart back on the road no doubt caused its share of panic attacks. But slowly, this artificial public relations campaign caught on with at least some of the movie-going public.

In films, the concept of benevolent biker had been breached as early as 1969 with the TV series *Then Came Bronson*, where Michael Park's wandering biker was depicted basically as one of the good guys. The simple formula of bikers entering a town, causing trouble, and eventually being confronted by the law would still be milked for years to come, but filmmakers were gradually waking up to the cash potential of portraying bikers as simple, everyman's heroes. The filthy, worn leathers that were considered the hallmark

Here, Bogdanovich chronicles the true story of Rocky Dennis, a Southern California biker's son afflicted with a rare, disfiguring bone disease. A breakthrough film, the sappy but ultimately fascinating drama provided a soft-edged interpretation of the life of motorcycle gang members. There were few orgies and showdowns with *the Man*, but plenty of the chronic unemployment, close friendships, and recreational drug use that characterize everyday outlaw biker life. At times, *Mask* reads more like a study of what drugs and irresponsible parenting can do to families than an exploration of biker gangs. Despite its sometimes overwhelming sentimentality, the film works to dispel several long-standing myths about bikers: There are no shared 'ol ladies, and no evidence of international drug distribution rings, for example, but all the characters seem to use the club for insulation from the outside world.

Film buffs will remember it was Bogdanovich who had served as a last-minute script writer, editor, and assistant to director Roger Corman on the 1966 biker movie classic *The Wild Angels*. By the time the director of the Oscar-winning *Last Picture Show* filmed *Mask* almost two decades later, the popular view of motorcycle gangs was very different from the one he and Corman had presented a generation before. Much of this movie's appeal comes from a believable, unpretentious script, written with assistance from Rusty Dennis, Rocky's real-life mother. A dyed-in-the-wool California biker, Rusty's plucky demeanor was captured in full by Cher, who, along with the ever-craggy Sam Elliott as Gar, made a convincing duo. Rocky is played with casual sincerity by Eric Stoltz, wearing enough stage makeup to outfit a *Planet Of The Apes* cast party.

Stoltz later starred in *Waterdance* (1992) where he portrayed a young novelist recovering from an accident in a hospital paraplegic ward with another outlaw biker, played to slimy perfection by William Forsythe.

In a clever re-tooling of a familiar biker movie scene where outlaw bikers are discriminated against for their non-conformist appearance, *Mask* includes a bit where Rocky's considerable physical deformity causes its own share of revulsion and prejudice from outside the biker community. When the bikers stick up for him, offering

of menace in films like 1967's *Devil's Angels*, were slowly coming to be perceived as the uniform of America's last great frontier heroes.

The "Easy Rider" generation's coming of age served as motivation for comic screenwriter Albert Brooks' mid-life crisis comedy, *Lost in America* (1985). Brooks plays the husband of Julie Haggerty. They're the quintessential 80s yuppie couple who decide to go off in search of "the real America, just like in *Easy Rider*." The pair encounter only one biker who pauses just long enough to sneer at their motor home before offering a one-finger salute. The couple end up having an only slightly less successful, but altogether more laughable, quest than Hopper and Fonda.

Another example of the maturing face of motorcycling was Peter Bogdanovich's *Mask* (1985).

mutual support in the face (no pun intended) of a serious disability, the film manages to display the most human side of bikers and their lifestyle. For good or bad, *Mask,* paved a stretch of cinematic highway for more good guy biker films.

Among the sillier of the new breed of biker movies was *Hog Wild* (1980), a Canadian spoof of outlaw biker movies starring Tony Rosato of *Saturday Night Live* fame; *Easy Wheels* (1986), an outrageous biker comedy where two gender-opposite gangs, the Bourne Losers and Women of the Wolf are set against each other by *Evil Dead* director David O'Malley; and *Masters of Menace* (1990).

Starring a crew of veteran film and television character actors including punk rock singer Lee Ving as Roy Boy and David "Squiggy" Lander from TV's *Laverne and Shirley, Masters of Menace* took the intimidation and casual violence out of motorcycle gangs and replaced it with a childish sense of mischief. Instead of bloody confrontations with townspeople, the Road Masters simply ride around on their Hogs visiting strip-tease bars and guzzling beers.

An uneven send-up of both biker movies and National Lampoon's frat-house comedy *Animal House, Masters* supplies enough juvenile references to the female anatomy to keep all but the most discriminating 14-year old in stitches. But even with Catherine Bach from television's *Dukes of Hazard* in a sexpot role as club leader Buddy Wheeler's (David Rasche) long-suffering ol' lady, the sex level never rises above a very Benny-Hill type voyeurism. Similarly, the Road Masters wear cut-off denim vests, drink too much beer, and ride a bad-ass column of choppers, though deep down they're nothing more than a college fraternity with beards; *Revenge of the Nerds* on Harleys, if you will.

Masters of Menace does manage to laugh at itself and the deadpan seriousness of many early biker movies by regurgitating a lot of standard-issue macho lines. Thankfully, the lines are delivered with the actors self-consciously winking at the camera.

When the gang is challenged to stay out of trouble for three years at the behest of an exceptionally cranky judge, the stage is set for all sorts of harmless shenanigans. Punch is made from

window cleaner, bikes are ridden into living rooms, and the Road Masters drink beer straight from the keg, but never do they appear more threatening than a pushy phone-solicitor.

Masters of Menace wasn't the first movie appearance of a bumbling, ineffectual motorcycle gang, however. In the early 1960s, a gang known as the Rats showed up to crash a number of Frankie Avalon and Annette Funicello's beach party films. The gang made several appearances, always fronted by Erik Von Zipper (Harvey Lembeck), a curiously middle-aged delinquent, intended as a send-up of Brando's Johnny from *The Wild One.*

More of this kind of biker surfaced a few years later in Clint Eastwood's jocular, tough-guy comedies *Every Which Way But Loose* (1978) and the similar sequel *Any Which Way You Can* (1980). Eastwood and his orangutan sidekick Clyde (as himself) fend off the feeble threats of the Black Widows, a Tacoma, Washington, motorcycle gang who are such poor brawlers they're chased off in one scene by an 80-year old, shotgun-wielding Ruth Gordon. Eastwood, himself a longtime biker, showed a genuine sense of humor and timeliness for his harmless portrayal of bikers, which contrasted sharply with the vicious cycle gang in *The Gauntlet* (1977). In this action-chase police adventure set in Arizona's Monument Valley, Eastwood is forced to confront and subdue an entire outlaw gang in order to steal one of their choppers. The role was typical for Eastwood in this period, as he would save then-wife Sondra Locke from the biker gang's amorous advances.

When filmmakers weren't busy de-fanging bikers, the later years also saw a return to utilizing thinly-veiled western formulas in biker movies, as with *Harley-Davidson and the Marlboro Man* (1991). This movie was notable, if for nothing else, as being the only film in history shameless enough to squeeze the names of not one, but two popular advertising icons into a single title. Starring actor-boxer-biker Mickey Rourke and Don Johnson from television's *Miami Vice,* it took the basic premise of Henry Fonda-Glen Ford buddy films into a weird, post-modern future where crooked corporate mergers and environmentally irresponsible land acquisition deals had replaced ranching as America's primary

Despite leading the cinema in shameless product name-placement, Mickey Rourke and Don Johnson's *Harley-Davidson and the Marlboro Man* **(1991) was a classic** on the road **buddy film in the tradition of Newman/Redford's** *Butch Cassidy and the Sundance Kid.* **(M.G.M.)**

commercial endeavor. Johnson, attired in a dusty cowpoke outfit apparently lifted from the set of *Bonanza,* does an admirable job of creating a luckless but lovable saddle tramp. With his wry, gallows humor and tattered Stetson, Johnson's cowboy-biker takes up the reins where world-weary, down-on-their-luck Western sidekicks left off.

The plot of *Harley-Davidson and the Marlboro Man* follows the two road partners as they embark on the by-now familiar task of saving a friend's business from a group of unconscionable developers. The yuppie-bad/biker-good analogy is quickly established by the tension surrounding scenes shot in the high-rise confines of the film's protagonist, played with slimy smugness by *Saving Private Ryan's* Tom Sizemore.

The starkness and corruption of the corporate world is quickly contrasted against the casual, multi-racial camaraderie exhibited by our heroes, easily establishing who the good guys are, despite Rourke and Johnson's obvious character flaws. *Working in an office makes you mean and unscrupulous, but riding a Hog makes you funny and sexy* could easily be this movie's motto.

An odd cast that combines professional wrestler Big John Studd as the henpecked husband of defrocked Miss America Vanessa Williams and Spike Lee regular Giancarlo Esposito as one of Rourke's barroom buddies adds to this film's very insider casting. It's reminiscent of the Rat Pack's *Oceans 11* (1966) where anybody hanging around the right Vegas circles when Sinatra decided to cast the film was given a job.

Fall behind on your taxes in real life and at best you'll risk an IRS audit. In films, these events have a way of precipitating all manner of vehicle chases, gunfights, and acts of bravery. In this respect, *Harley-Davidson and the Marlboro Man* is no exception.

When Harley and The Marlboro Man rob an armored car to raise funds to save the bar they "practically grew up in" (owned by "The Old Man" played by veteran character actor Julius Harris) the pair discover their deed has netted them not cash, but millions of dollars worth of something called "Crystal Dream." This new wonder drug is taking to the streets faster than a crack high, and the rightful owners want it back.

While our heroes' flawless sense of morality doesn't prevent them from bedding a pair of married women, they disdain pushing the drugs themselves, deciding instead to blackmail the pushers. Unfortunately, these pushers are a robotic team of ultra-yuppies who arrive cloaked in tastefully-designed, bullet-proof, black leather overcoats. Led by Daniel Baldwin, the pushers stalk Rourke and Johnson with the steely determination of Arnold Schwarzenegger's Terminator.

At times, *Harley-Davidson and the Marlboro Man* is pretty funny with its corny barroom philosophizing; "Never chase women. Or busses," Johnson warns Rourke. The Paul Newman-Robert Redford western *Butch Cassidy and the Sundance Kid* (1969) is thoroughly mined for gags here as the two are forced to evade pursuers by jumping, not from a rocky cliff into rapids, but from the upper floors of a Los Angeles high-rise into a swimming pool. And like Newman-Redford, one partner is hamstrung by an inability to fire a handgun proficiently while the other can practically spell his name on his opponent's chest in gunshot wounds. Oddly, neither Harley nor the Marlboro Man realize their opponent's heads are not bullet proof like their jackets until the film's conclusion. For the most part, *Harley-Davidson and the Marlboro Man* could have easily been a Western with the simple exchange of tumbleweeds for skyscrapers and horses for Harleys. But instead of being appreciated as an over-the-top parody of the western genre, *Harley-Davidson and the Marlboro Man* was roundly derided by critics (for its title, among other things) although in recent years, it's come to be appreciated for what it is: a lighthearted buddy film that didn't take itself very seriously.

By now, seeing inoffensive, believable portrayals of bikers on screen and TV was old hat. James Brolin, a lifelong motorcycle enthusiast, gave motorcycling one of its earliest shots in the arm when he appeared as Dr. Steven Kiley, the handsome Dr. Motorcycle on TV's *Marcus Welby M.D.* in the early 1970s. Brolin later appeared as an everyday family man who rode a Yamaha triple in

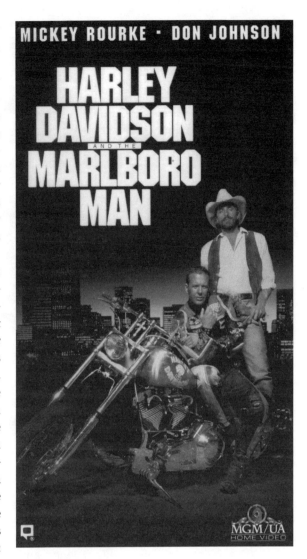

The Amityville Horror (1979). At the same time, *Lords of Flatbush* star Henry Winkler's character, Arthur "The Fonz" Fonzarelli made hoodlums almost lovable in TV's long-running sitcom *Happy Days.* While at the movies, Adian Quinn did a fair turn as a millhunk anti-hero riding a beat-up Honda in *Reckless* (1984). Quinn's confused young biker, caught in a dismal industrial town, was yet another extension of Brando's misunderstood hoodlum with the kind heart.

The very next year, even comedian Pee-Wee Herman stumbled into a biker club hangout in *Pee-Wee's Big Adventure* (1985) emerging unscathed after he earns the respect of an outlaw gang for his dedication to his bicycle and the road. Further credibility of the "Easy Rider" generation came on a 1986 episode of the popular

By the 1990s, even comedy stars like Steve "Police Academy" Guttenberg could assume the biker role for dramatic effect. In the romantic comedy *Don't Tell Her It's Me*, Guttenberg is reincarnated as a womanizing, macho Harley rider. (Sovereign Pictures)

CBS TV detective serial *Simon and Simon*. Here, Gerald MacRaney, the older, wiser member of the Simon clan, reveals his biker past, a period where he dressed in brown suede with fringes and "searched for America" on a chopper. This period was so open to inoffensive portrayals of bikers that comedic actor Steve Guttenberg re-invented himself as a jazzy, Beat-generation outrider in the romantic comedy *Don't Tell Her It's Me* (1990). In addition to a wider representation of movie and TV bikers, the variety of motorcycles "on screen at a theater or drive-in near you," to coin an old movie advertisement, were also broadening. Look for Italian Ducati 916s in *Fled* (1996) starring real-life Ducatisti Larry Fishburne, and a pair of new Triumphs in *Mission Impossible II* (2000) starring Tom Cruise.

Curiosity about the biker mystique also led to several made-for-TV documentary films about the outlaw legend. Films like the Arts and Entertainment Network's *Secret Life of Outlaw Bikers* (1999), MTV's *Road Hogs* (1992), the Discovery Channels *Choppers* (2000), and *Hell's Angels* (1999) all shared an uncritical, historical view of outlaw bikers, presenting them as mythic figures instead of villains. These documentaries, like most biker films, ignored most everything but the hard-core Harley scene, but at least they weren't as consumed by tales of crime and debauchery as earlier biker documentaries like *It's A Revolution, Mother* (1969) and *Hell's Angels Forever* (1982).

The video rental revolution of the 1980s also aided biker movies immensely. As more moviegoers were watching films on their VCR's rather than in theaters, low-budget filmmakers were given a reprieve from major-release financing where budgets would include posters, lobby cards, multiple prints, etc. Instead, low-budget biker movies and action flicks could amass handsome rental figures using little more than provocative tape covers and minimal advertising.

In this climate, its no surprise that movie studios continued with the proven formula of the outlaw with the heart of gold. A trio of other films which touched on nearly identical formulas of aging or benevolent outlaw bikers included: The made-for-TV *Return of the Rebels* (1981) starring Barbara "I Dream of Jeannie" Eden, *Running Cool* (1993), which cast a crew of hard-partying bikers against an unfriendly southern town and its environmentally-incorrect land developers, and *Chrome Soldiers* (1992), which followed a group of Vietnam Veteran bikers with a flair for detective work.

Although these films were made some ten years apart, they portrayed themes of camaraderie and brotherhood among bikers as a positive, rather than a threatening facet of the motorcycle gang code. And again, the formula for converting bikers into heroes was clear and quite simple: suits were evil, and bikers, the new knights of the highways, could reluctantly be persuaded out of the saddle or saloon long enough to right the occasional wrong.

In *Return of the Rebels*, ex-biker mamma Barbara Eden is Mary Beth Allen, who runs an Eagle Rock California lakeside resort. The place is overrun by a crew of unruly teenagers, led by a young Patrick Swayze. Rather than blink them into the next dimension as Major Nelson would have suggested, Mary Beth instead calls on her former biker buddies for help—among them, the unlikely casting of Jamie Farr, the cross-dressing Corporal Klinger of TV's *M*A*S*H* and veteran actor Don Murray. In a story guaranteed to appeal to Baby-Boomer audiences, the old crew, all of whom have become rather successful and pudgy middle-aged businessmen, decide to risk their comfortable careers and Stairmaster lifestyles for one last weekend of biking and brawling.

Heretofore bikers were, with rare exception, youthful hell raisers whose athletic prowess was always at near-Tarzan levels. *Return of the Rebels*, for the first time, addresses the uncomfortable fact that many first generation bikers were, by the early 1980s, growing a little long in the beard.

The Eagle Rock Rebels show up dressed quite accurately as 1950s bikers: black leather jackets with hand-painted logos, high-cuffed jeans, and Brando caps. Even their Harleys are built to

STEVE GUTTENBERG
JAMI GERTZ
KYLE MACLACHLAN
AND
SHELLEY LONG
as Lizzie

DON'T TELL HER IT'S ME

A HILARIOUS COMEDY ABOUT TRUE LOVE AND FALSE IDENTITY

conform to post-WWII Bob-Job specs, with plenty of flat black paint, solo saddles and fishtail exhausts. The club's initial attempts to take to the road result in some seriously bad riding, with the obviously uncomfortable actors genuinely struggling to master controls of their unruly vintage Harleys.

A group of younger outlaws force the Rebels off the road in one sequence, and they respond by complaining about lower back pain and threatening to retreat to the office instead of risking several weeks in traction by playing biker. With the film's only violence saved for its predictable climax, *Return of the Rebels* is a harmless and thoroughly enjoyable exercise in biker nostalgia. Of course it's odd that the Rebels still fit into their old club leathers some 20 years after seeing any road

western archive, the made-for-cable *Chrome Soldiers* stars Gary Busey, Ray Sharkey, and Yaphett Koto as a group of war vets (this time Vietnam and Desert Storm) who visit yet another corrupt small town to investigate the murder of Busey's older brother. As Busey and crew emerge from a fight with a gang of local rednecks, they groan and wobble like veterans at a Major League Baseball Hall of Fame game, their age obviously catching up with them.

Things move fast in this film, but few things zip about as recklessly as Yaphett (star of NBC TV's *Homicide* series) Koto's badly placed toupee, an obvious and distracting hairpiece which seems to be covering a different part of his head in each shot. The toothy and gregarious Busey, who suffered a head injury from an erred, helmetless stunt aboard his own Harley just months before production, is noted for wearing a helmet throughout the film.

Far different from typical screen bikers and very 1990s in temperament, Busey and company are mature enough to shuck out of their leathers long enough to dress formally for a friend's funeral. They also behave politely around women and back the cops off, not with broken noses and chain-whippings, but with the very real threat of a class action lawsuit.

Further distancing these Harley riders from traditional roles is an odd line of dialogue delivered by Busey as the troubled "Flash." He denies being a member of a biker gang, defending his lifestyle with the cop-out, "We're not bikers. The bikes were just a form of therapy after we got home from Nam."

Among this crew of "non-bikers" is an attorney, a stockbroker, a rancher, and a veteran military pilot—all of whom manage to circumvent careers and family long enough to investigate the murder of Stoney, Flash's older brother who refused to play ball with a group of drug-distributing cops. If the irony of bikers fighting a group of filthy, drug-dealing cops isn't weird enough, Nick Randall's up-to-now believable screenplay includes an improbable ending where the gang brings justice via a successful plea to the Feds for an investigation of police corruption.

This was enough to make any real life outlaw wonder if Captain America, The Wild One, and

use. And when the club tells the vicious teen gang leader (Swayze) that the Rebels were probably just like him in their glory days, it's an interesting example of one generation's rebellion being lost on the next.

Regardless of being overly idealistic, movies like this were some of the cleverest enticements ever devised for aging former riders to get back in the saddle. With mortgages and steady employment beckoning, *Return of the Rebels* not only told people who hadn't ridden a motorcycle in decades to try it again, it proved another step towards humanizing bikers in the cinema.

Continuing to follow a group of riders who are more likely to contract lower back pain than syphilis is *Chrome Soldiers* (1992). Using yet another plot vulcanized from Hollywood's dense

Sonny Barger himself hadn't gone off the deep end and traded in their engineer boots and denim vests for Hush Puppies and cardigan sweaters. Before the triumphant, militaristic soundtrack bleats its last chord, *Chrome Soldiers*, which one can only suppose was aimed more at patriotic, god-fearing veterans than real bikers, ends with the gang receiving a standing ovation from the townsfolk for their good deeds.

Coincidentally, *Chrome Soldiers*, borrows some of its ideas from 1968's *Chrome and Hot Leather*, which featured a surprisingly adept performance from soul singer Marvin Gaye. Here, Gaye and a trio of his bike-riding buddies fresh from Vietnam face off against a cycle gang led by biker movie regular William Smith, to avenge the murder of one soldier's fiancee.

Ending the trio of biker-as-hero films is *Running Cool*, a movie that suffered at the box office by being released at nearly the same time as, and with a similar title to, Disney's comedy about the Jamaican Olympic bobsled team, *Cool Runnings*. An interesting and very 1990s movie, *Running Cool* presented what could be considered the screen's first ecologically aware Green Party bikers. While these Harley riders rode and partied as hard as any other movie bikers, *Running Cool* showed the gentle, natural side of the Harley crowd, the kind of bikers who would rather wax sentimental over the plight of the endangered Speckled Whooping Crane than guzzle beers in a backwoods saloon.

Filmed in part at Sturgis, *Running Cool* provides us with yet another visit to a corrupt small southern town, a locale that all movie bikers seem inexorably drawn toward, despite its viciousness. In this instance, an aging biker, Iron Butt Garrett—who's brought to life by the gruff character actor James Gammon—is about to lose his South Carolina wetlands hideaway to a greedy land developer played with typical smug authority by Calvin Hogg, a/k/a Paul "The Breakfast Club" Gleason.

The story's sentimentality and corny platitudes toward naturalism may come off a bit clumsy, but the film has proven popular with the Harley crowd for its homey, outback charm. Directors Beverly and Ferd Sebastian's portrayal of business people as unconscionable and cowardly

and anyone with a beard or tattoos as inherently heroic has also found an audience. When the beefy hero Bones (Andrew Divoff) falls for Dee Dee Pfeiffer's Michelle, a pretty, handicapped waitress, it echoes Brando's falling for a square chick way back in *The Wild One*. Bones is serious from the start, first slapping a couple of customers around for flirting with Michelle, then later, convincing his bros to build his new lady a custom Harley trike. With the romance fully established, courtesy of a tearful confession of how Bones lost his family to a drunk driver, the bros get down to the business of straightening out the money-hungry yuppies. Not that the bikers in *Running Cool* are above a good rumble—the opening scene has Bear (Bubba Baker) and Bones scaring off a biker intent on starting a knife fight

They were the last thing this town ever wanted...

But just what it needed.

RUNNING COOL

in a Sturgis bar. The biker's constant confrontations with Hogg's son Blue (Tracy Sebastian) and an inept team of hired henchmen get good and violent at times, but it never ends without a light-hearted conclusion. After one tangle with the bikers, Hogg's men are left naked and covered in poison ivy in the back of a pickup truck parked in the town square. And with no calamine lotion to boot!

To further develop the biker's "aw shucks, we just want to ride and party" nature, Hogg offers the brothers $200,000 for the opportunity to transform their picturesque marshland into a working soy-bean farm. With all the believability of a *Penthouse* magazine letter, the bikers decline, opting instead to stage a charity "Wetlands Run," where

they'll use the proceeds to pay the back taxes owed on the land.

Of course, this isn't out of the question for a group of hard-core Harley riders who like to cuddle baby pigs, threaten people with squirt guns, and stare at wildlife with a poignancy and seriousness that would make John Audobon proud. How this would play in real life is anybody's guess.

At one point, Bones, on his way to woo Michelle—whose previously pitiful leg brace now looks pretty bitchin' matched with her new leather Harley-chick threads—pauses just long enough to free a pelican from entanglement in a thicket.

With its wholesale, albeit patronizing endorsement of everything bikers are reputed to hold dear, *Running Cool* did everything it could to ensure its popularity among the people it depicted, that is, short of offering free Harleys at each screening. By the end of the film, the bikers have predictably won over the townsfolk, successfully initiated not only the town's outcast crippled girl and two randy old ladies into their ranks, but they've successfully derailed a multi-million dollar land development deal. Not too bad for a group of guys who, in movies from just ten or twenty years before, couldn't stop fighting amongst themselves long enough to stay out of prison.

However, making bikers cuddly and easy to like could have its drawbacks, Hollywood seemed to say. Producing a film that helped audiences realize that the private lives of most bikers were every bit as predictable as their own was a bit of a risk considering the excitement and raw sexuality moviegoers had come to expect from anybody on two wheels. If filmmakers unwittingly displayed bikers as real people rather than modern-day outlaws who lived strictly for the existential thrill, would the Maximum Angel suddenly become Fred "Father Knows Best" MacMurray in leathers?

Well, not exactly.

The 80s and 90s still saw plenty of unflattering film portrayals of bikers as everything from vampires in *Samurai Vampire Bikers from Hell* (1992), to foul-smelling bounty-hunters in *Raising Arizona* (1985), to white supremacist terrorists *Dead Bang*

(1989). All these portrayals ensured few people would ever mistake the one-percenter down the block with Mister Rogers. And though bikers still made for convincing villains and movie monsters, the one biker role that proved most popular with filmmakers and moviegoing audiences was that of the biker-as-cop. The multiple roles of detectives, moral guardians, and police officers that Busey, Koto, and Sharkey adopt in *Chrome Soldiers*, proved a well movie makers returned to again and again in recent years.

It also provided an excuse for a phenomenal display of macho posturing and self-possessed studliness for NCAA star linebacker-cum-actor Brian Bosworth in the outlandish *Stone Cold* (1991). Filled with buxom, bare-breasted women, vicious, cop-killing bikers, and dialogue that seemed oddly dated by the time of its big-screen release, *Stone Cold* was an odd mix of classic biker exploitation movie and predictable, renegade-cop-who-makes-his-own-rules formulas. It's not clear who the intended audience for this movie was; Bosworth, who had bombed in his rookie NFL season with the Seattle Seahawks was, by then, on the media's list of persona non gratis. Meanwhile, few genuine bikers could be expected to line up to see a movie where only the ugliest sides of their lifestyles were exaggerated almost beyond recognition.

That audiences—particularly the editors of biker magazines like New York City's *Iron Horse*—objected to the murderous, mafia-styled bikers in *Stone Cold* rather than the neo-detective bikers that Busey and company had portrayed in *Chrome Soldiers* revealed how sensitive bikers had become about how the media portrayed them.

After watching the movie, it was hard to blame them. With the overly-macho characters depicted by actor William Forsythe as gang enforcer and a very craggy-looking Lance Henriksen as the grizzled gang leader "Chains," *Stone Cold* was rife with the sort of outlaw biker stereotyping of a generation before. Scenes shot inside the club compound of The Brotherhood, a fictitious Mississippi one-percenter gang, are a montage of intentionally scary and lurid scenery: naked women showering outdoors, a hilariously over-the-top rendition of a biker funeral pyre, bikers guarding elaborate towers with automatic rifles,

College football all-star linebacker Brian Bosworth takes his turn in the saddle as undercover cop John Stone in the over-the-top biker epic *Stone Cold* (1991). (Columbia Pictures)

sinewy Dobermans patrolling the gates and enough gratuitous sneering to fuel a World Wrestling Federation press conference. Veteran screenwriter and executive producer Walter Doniger seems to have been influenced heavily by Canadian writer Yves Lavigne's true-crime novel *Hell's Angels: Three Can Keep a Secret If Two Are Dead*. There's plenty of comic-book violence, with the Brotherhood killing a federal prosecutor with a bomb, tossing grenades around as casually as Harleys leak oil, and one far-fetched bit where members shoot beer cans off each other's heads with machine guns. These scenes in *Stone Cold* are presented with about as much believability as a Jackie Chan fight scene, though some of these incidents were based in fact. They had been

police officer who volunteers to help the F.B.I. infiltrate a notorious outlaw biker gang. Sheen, always brooding and on the edge, puts in a consistent performance as Dan Saxon, a young undercover cop who, we learn through a series of vague, shadowy flashbacks, was severely abused by his father. The release of *Beyond The Law* was delayed for almost three years after its completion due to some serious distribution problems. This left the film's premiere to cable TV, where it was broadcast during the kind of late hours that only a Hollywood gadfly like Charlie Sheen himself is reportedly awake. As a theatrical release, *Beyond The Law* might have fared well with fans of mysteries and cop flicks because, unlike other movies from the biker-cop genre, this film relies more on the tensions of maintaining an undercover persona, and less on the crashing bikes, gunfights, and exploding cop cars we'd expect to find in this type of movie.

The script is also helped along considerably by a supporting cast of up-and-coming young actors and actresses, including Linda Fiorentino as Renee, Saxon's conflicted photographer girlfriend, Courtney B. Vance as Conroy Prince, a straightlaced government agent, and Michael Madsen, the notorious Mr. Pink from Quentin Tarantino's *Reservoir Dogs* in an appropriately slimy role as Blood, leader of the biker gang. Sheen's conflicted cop is drawn into the undercover role, where, in the course of procuring several stashes of illegal weaponry and enough methamphetamine to wire a thoroughbred, Saxon starts getting confused about where his characterization ends and where the dark side of life begins. He must commit a wider and increasingly heinous series of crimes to remain in the gang's good graces and complete his mission, but can he turn back when there's free crank, whiskey, and violence with no consequences? With its lawless, evil bike gang, *Beyond The Law* is proof that the old biker movie formulas can still prove entertaining, even in the face of an increasingly politically correct view of bikers. For what it's worth, *Beyond The Law* is not an entirely bad take on the genre and contains one of Sheen's better performances.

Movie fans who scour the shelves of their local video stores for obscure titles might want to check

committed in one way or another by real outlaw gangs in the US and Europe as they competed with traditional organized crime families for control of drug and prostitution rackets in the late 80s and early 90s. Factual or not, Bosworth received some pretty derisive reviews for his first big screen outing. Despite rooming with a giant pet lizard whom Bosworth is forced to make conversation with, he's no worse at the maverick cop role than a thousand actors before and after him.

The maverick biker lawman who rides into a den of evil and corruption and straighten things out theme was worked to similar effect in *Beyond The Law* (1992), a star vehicle for actor Charlie Sheen. *Beyond the Law* (titled *Fixing the Shadow* on video release) was a reasonably well-acted, mid-budget, undercover cop thriller about a lone out a quartet of low-budget action features by writer-director-star Jason Williams. Born blonde, hunky, and possessing a profile more angular than Arizona's Monument Valley (where these and many other biker movies and westerns were filmed) Williams launched his Hog-mounted bounty hunter Wade Olsen in *Danger Zone* (1987). These B-movie, video store staples quickly generated something of a cult following, prompting Williams to produce *Danger Zone II: Reaper's Revenge*(1988), *Danger Zone III: Steel Horse War* (1990), and *Danger Zone IV* (1992). William's quartet of biker-cop-westerns contain little in the way of new cinematic technique and the cast of unknowns seems comprised mainly of stunt men, out-of-work centerfold models, and a few real bikers.

Most of the series is consumed with our hero tracking an outlaw gang across the desert on his trusty Shovelhead. In the process, Williams' Wade Olsen gets to utter cornball lines like "I've got a date with the devil," as he defeats the odds—and about 30, foul-looking, drug-addled guys twice his size—before riding off into the proverbial sunset. Yeah, it plays like an episode of *Gunsmoke* without even the trusty Festus available for sidekick comic relief, but *Danger Zone III,* the series' clear best, lacks nothing for viewers searching for a 90-minute blast of mindless macho adventure.

It's highly unlikely we've seen the last combination cop/biker drama, given the relative (video rental) success of the *Danger Zone* series and Lorenzo Lamas' similarly-themed TV series *Renegade.* This series, now in syndication, proved that America's appetite for lonely, handsome heroes, riding through a vanishing frontier, hadn't changed much since the days of John Wayne, only this time his horse was running on 40-weight, not oats.

For all of the negative stereotypes about motorcyclists the outlaw biker movies created and occasionally helped maintain, the chopper dramas of the 1960s are today seen mostly as harmless pop culture period pieces. Enough time has passed since *The Devil's Angels* were considered threatening, and it's unlikely a biker's boss and his next-door neighbors formed their opinions of him from something they saw at the drive-in. Chances are, they hold a favorable opinion of bikers, and there's a strong possibility this had something to do with revisionist biker movies like *Running Cool* and *Mask.*

With more than a half-century of biker movies in print, there's a varied enough catalogue of work—depicting riders as good guys, weird guys, and everything in between—that motorcyclists no longer have to worry that they're going to be lumped in with outlaws and movie monsters just because they ride a bike.

For the most part, today's sophisticated, media-savvy public can tell the difference between movie sensationalism and truth, a development that couldn't have come too soon for most bikers. For good or bad, all of these films have become part of motorcycling history. Like every family photo album, there will be shots we'd rather not look at and some we can't tear ourselves away from. I'm just glad someone was there to take the pictures.

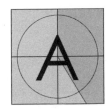

Resource Guide

Finding biker movies can be easy. One of the most complete sources is Whitehorse Press, the publisher of this book. The movie section of their free motorcycling catalog lists more than fifty (some hard to find) titles. You can also try your local video store. Most major chains such as Blockbuster or Hollywood Video and smaller, independent video rental shops carry at least a few of the better-known biker movies, though the more obscure titles often show up in little out-of-the-way stores and through vendors working at motorcycle trade shows and swap meets.

Thanks to the internet, locating long out-of-print and foreign titles on VHS cassette means simply logging on to a popular search engine like Lycos or Yahoo. Comprehensive listings of casts, characters, and production cross-references can be found, along with a guide to which movies, posters, and memorabilia are available at The Internet Movie Database (imdb.com).

Many biker movies from the 1960s have been re-released in recent years, some containing rare trailers not seen since the films showed in first-run movie houses. Keep in mind, foreign movies are typically released in the PAL format which will not work in a VCR manufactured in the US. Transfer services are available at video imaging labs, but can be expensive.

Critic's Choice Video
P.O. Box 749
Itasca, IL. 60143-0749
(800) 544-9852
www.ccvideo.com

International Film and Video Center
991 First Ave.
New York, NY. 10022
(212) 826-8848

Movies Unlimited
6736 Castor Ave.
Philadelphia, PA. 19149
(800) 523-0823
www.moviesunlimited.com

Whitehorse Press
P.O. Box 60
North Conway, NH. 03860-0060
(800) 531-1133
www.WhitehorsePress.com

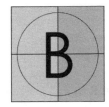

Movie Reviews

Selecting a favorite biker movie is not much different from choosing a custom motorcycle in that everyone's tastes are different. Therefore, anyone looking to start a personal library of biker movies should pick a little of everything. Film critics tend to favor *Easy Rider* and *The Wild One* above all others as the best of the genre, and while both of these films were seminal works of their respective periods, filled with quality acting and timeless cool, many of the lesser-known, low-budget features contain memorable images from biking's history. True, *Harley's Angels* may not have won any awards for witty scripting or dazzling camera work, but these straight-to-drive-in movies that often starred real life bikers playing themselves provide some of the big screen's most accurate depictions of two-wheeled life.

Following is a list of some of my favorite biker movies, rated in no particular order. Varying in historical perspective and location, they provide both casual viewers and collectors alike with a broad, comprehensive view of the motorcycle subculture. Each of the ten films selected are currently available on videotape (see resource guide). Watch all of them singularly or in an all-day orgy of popcorn and black leather and you'll no doubt be ready to get you motor runnin' and head out on the highway.

The Loveless (1983)
Director Kathryn Bigelow
Starring Willem Dafoe, Robert Gordon
One of the best-kept secrets in biker movies, this retro-cool look at biking in the 1950s is a far cry from the usual *Happy Days* portrayal of the period. Considered slow and arty by some, and a virtually plotless excuse to showcase some innovative camera techniques by others, *The Loveless* is one biker movie that manages to say more with images and subtle attitude than it does with words. Where else, for instance, can you watch a five-minute sequence of a greaser meticulously combing his DA and sideburns? Where else can vintage Harley-Davidson Panheads and Sportsters be viewed in all their fat-fendered glory? And few movies capture the alienation and outsider status bikers experienced in the 1950s as fully as does *The Loveless*. Deliberate, snail-paced shots of cheesecake shop calendars, antique roadside diners, and women in razor-sharp push-up bras and spike heels only add to the ambience of a movie that's been analyzed and deconstructed relentlessly in university film courses since its release. Despite more loose ends than a worn-out wiring harness (how, for example, did Gordon's character, the manic Davis, manage to avoid execution in the electric chair?)

Kathryn Bigelow's slow-paced film manages to pack plenty of poignant social commentary into its brief, 84-minute run, addressing issues of prison rehabilitation segregation (the bikers featured are all former cell mates from a Detroit penitentiary), the Red Scare, and even incest. A dedicated cult following has grown around this movie, with fans of 50s rock and roll and singer-actor Robert Gordon (who does a mean impression of rockabilly legend Carl Perkins) finding its edgy soundtrack of particular appeal.

The Wild One (1954)
Director Laszlo Benedek
Starring Marlon Brando, Lee Marvin, Mary Murphy, Jay C. Flippen

This is the movie that *The Loveless* and about half of all biker movies in existence have struggled—and mostly failed—to emulate. It's been a half century since Marlon Brando and Lee Marvin faced off for a weekend of small-town drinking and brawling and, despite some cheesy dialogue, *The Wild One* still maintains its rebellious edge. This is mainly due to a script that manages to convey some serious 1950s anti-social angst while seldom becoming overly serious (the late-night make-out scene between Brando and Mary Murphy aside). Having a horde of beer-swilling city boys on loud motorbikes invade a small town to blow off steam was scary stuff back in 1954—seen today, the public panic *The Wild One* caused seems hard to believe. Overall, from the crazy scat-singing and street drag races the gangs participate in, the whole melee now looks like a lot of fun. Watch closely and you'll see that *The Wild One* contains the initial examples of just about every biker movie cliche known to man: the bikes being ridden into the small-town saloon; the naive country girls who crave attention from the invading biker gang (when they should know better); and the screen's first appearance of an outlaw gang leader with a heart of gold concealed under layers of black leather and bravado. There's also a few historically significant moments, notably, a scene where a clean-cut biker attempts to distance himself from the "outlaw outfits" who disrupt sanctioned races, drink too much, and generally make life hard for other bikers. Scenes like these go a long way toward explaining the origins of the whole outlaw biker concept, plus, they're a blast to watch. Trivia buffs might want to look for the last name of Brando's Johnny, mentioned only once in the entire film.

Once a Jolly Swagman (1948)
Director Jack Lee
Starring Dirk Bogarde, Bonar Colleno

On a level of pure cinematography, this post-WWII drama about British motorcycle racing stands out above all. Filmed in an era when multi-angle camera techniques and floating dolly shots were still years away, Lee manages to get right under the helmet visor of his vintage speedway racers with shots that capture all the grit, glory, and determination of motorcycle racing. Shot mostly at night at several dirt tracks in the UK, *One A Jolly Swagman* takes on a dreamlike quality as the racers seem to exist only in a twilight world of fast bikes and deadly risks. This is a motorcycle racing movie first and foremost, but the 88-minute drama succeeds on levels other than the visual as well. Bogarde's portrayal of an idealistic racer who is determined to win decent wages and checkered flags for his team is flawless, as are several supporting roles provided by Bill Owen and Renee Asherton. The subject matter is obscure, but within the dejected veteran riders and the fearless young upstarts, there are characters here that nearly any biker can identify with. You'll have to look long and hard to find a copy of this one which is only recently receiving widespread video release, but the search is well worth it.

Hell's Angels Forever (1983)
Director Richard Chase
Documentary

"This time, the Hell's Angels decided to tell their own story, their own way," says the voice-over introduction on this self-made documentary by the notorious outlaw gang. The statement leads viewers to believe they're in for some stirring, never-before-revealed insight into the inner-sanctum of outlaw bike clubs. Instead, the Hell's Angels spend a fortune making a movie that does little to dispel the public's fear and misunderstanding of outlaw bikers. Nearly every one of the candid anecdotes the club members include involves "punching somebody in the head." Or hitting somebody with a hammer. Or drawing a gun on a friend. Whatever. If all of this casual mayhem was intended to be humorous, it's about as funny as a broken jaw. In the course of this movie's graphic 92-minute run, we're treated to live footage of several. Anyone harboring romantic notions about biker gangs need only watch this one from start to finish for a real insider's look at how much casual violence and brain-numbing drug use really goes on within the fold. There are a few redeeming moments, but you've got to endure a fair share of ugly to find them. Highlights include lengthy footage of long columns of radical Harley choppers (most of the film was shot during the mid- to late 1970s). Nearly every time one of the scraggly club members speaks to the interviewers on camera, they manage to goof-up the moment, either by waxing self-reverential ("the only thing I could compare this to is ancient Greek or Roman warrior societies" one member says, and with a straight face, no less), or by talking with all the bravado of professional wrestlers. Another highlight is the music: a breezy, hippie-rock and honky-tonk soundtrack from Johnny Paycheck, Bo Didley, and former Grateful Dead frontman Jerry Garcia helps to create the feeling that viewers have accidentally dropped in on one hell of a party. But this party all too often ends with someone, somewhere, getting smashed over the head for reasons known only to the filmmakers and subjects. Still, without the Angels willing to open themselves up to the world in this oft-misunderstood documentary, with all the warts, bail bondsmen, and extended prison stays included, people would still view them as folk heroes. Instead, *Hell's Angels Forever* once and for all reveals the Angels for what they are—true outlaws and fully, seriously, apart from the rest of mainstream society.

Quadrophenia (1979)
Director Franc Rodman
Starring Phil Daniels, Sting, Leslie Ash

A sense of belonging and group identity are themes played out again and again in biker movies, but seldom as well as in this British release. Set in 1964 during the peak seasons for Mods versus Rockers confrontations throughout England, *Quadrophenia* is the well-scripted brainchild of members of the rock supergroup The Who. Roger Daltrey, Keith Moon, Pete Townsend, and John Entwistle culled the screenplay from personal recollections and news events that occurred during their own teen years—which must have been one hell of a wild ride. At times, this 114-minute feature film contains the best parts of *West Side Story*, *The Wild One*, and the Beatles' *Hard Days Night*, shifting focus from a serious coming-of-age drama to a long-form music video. Quadrophenia chronicles a few weeks in the life of Jimmy (Daniels) a bright kid who seems intent on throwing it all away—job, future, and family—in order to be part of the Mods, a scooter-riding pack of pill-popping kids from the suburbs. This is one of the few biker movies that looks at why and how people join subcultures. There are also plenty of bikes present, mostly vintage Triumphs and the like. The price Jimmy pays for a sense of belonging calls the whole shebang into question, though the real joy in *Quadrophenia* is watching a youth movement in all its nihilistic, self-destructive glory. A soundtrack of original music by The Who creates a perfect feel for the time, though first-time viewers might be put off by the cast's working class British accents, which are harder to decipher than London fog.

The Wild Angels (1966)
Director Roger Corman
Starring Bruce Dern, Peter Fonda, Diane Ladd, Nancy Sinatra

As groundbreaking in its day as *The Wild One* had been a decade before, *The Wild Angels* was American International Pictures' first foray into the biker movie genre. Generating dozens of imitators and plenty of box-office, *The Wild Angels* was easily one of the studio's best efforts. Sparse on dialogue, but long on vivid riding sequences, this movie set the standard for biker gang pictures that followed. Besides a need to bury Dern's character Loser, who loses it all during a chase on a stolen police bike, the film's flimsy plot centers around finding a place for the bikers to party.

Basically, this serves as the same motivation for numerous biker movies, but this was the first of its kind. The movie starts off with Fonda and Dern portraying some fairly believable biker-lifestyle problems: they're in trouble with the landlord and having a hard time holding onto their day jobs. By the end of *The Wild Angels'* 93 minutes, the guys seem to have given up on attempts at living a normal life and let things devolve into an orgy of broken beer bottles and flying fists. Moody and at times genuinely creepy, director Corman's rough-hewn classic manages to convey the sexual threat of motorcycle gangs who, here, seem as intent on raping as riding. Custom bike fans can catch some excellent shots of early California customs in action; Fonda's Fat Bob Panhead a clear inspiration for many factory-custom bikes that would emerge decades later.

On Any Sunday (1971)
Director Bruce Brown
Documentary starring Steve McQueen, Mert Lawwill

This is the feature-length sales brochure the motorcycle industry should have made. Fortunately for them, former surfing enthusiast Bruce Brown concocted a documentary that was an exhilarating incitement to join the two-wheeled brotherhood. Much has changed since Brown won an Academy Award for chronicling the careers of the country's top motorcycle competitors and everyday riders—the hairstyles and clothes included. But the bare-bones, box-van-and-a-roll-of-duct-tape racing operations conducted by champion AMA riders in those days lends *On Any Sunday* a charming quaintness, especially when compared to the corporate-sponsored money machines that occupy starting grids on modern racetracks. This isn't the glamorous life of World Superbike—most of these racers are blasting along the track nursing painful injuries suffered in previous races. This movie's depiction of motorcycling as a wholesome pastime the whole family could enjoy stood in stark contrast to the outlaw biker images that were so popular on movie screens during the late 60s and early 70s. This helped make *On Any Sunday* one of the first (and only) motorcycle movies embraced by the mainstream media. Granted, some of Brown's off-road riding sequences with their silly flute soundtrack music sound especially dated today and several carry on far too long. But the filmmaker captures some hairy on-track action through his all-encompassing lens that brings the dangers of professional motorcycle racing startlingly to life, even on the small screen. Brown missed little during his filming, taking in hill climbs, dirt track racing, motocross, and road racing.

Eat The Peach (1986)
Director Peter Ormond
Starring Stephen Brennan, Eamon Morrissey

Little has been revealed about motorcycling in Ireland, a country where two-wheeled travel enjoys a healthy tradition. Released in 1987, *Eat The Peach* is a thoroughly enjoyable tale about two Irish bikers who try and make a living from their passion for motorbikes. Here, viewers get a rare look at the men and women who make their careers from riding bikes professionally, the disappointments, and the chronically empty gas tanks and bank accounts. Reportedly based on a true story, *Eat The Peach* lets viewers in on the secrets and struggles involved in staging a traveling stunt show. Sidetracked briefly by an unimportant sub-plot concerning whiskey smugglers and organized crime, *Eat The Peach* is the rare biker movie content to make the bike riders out to be everyday Joes with everyday problems, not macho supermen. Imbued with that uniquely morose, self-deprecating Irish sense of humor, *Eat The Peach* can make viewers grow genuinely concerned with how things work out for the pair of riders. If Evel Kneivel's trio of films had centered on the problems his death-defying career caused for his family instead of the motorcycle jumps themselves, they might have had the uniquely human touch that *Eat The Peach* does.

Easy Rider (1969)
Director Dennis Hopper
Starring Peter Fonda, Dennis Hopper, Jack Nicholson

This movie has been imitated ad nauseum and covered front to back by film critics over the years, and despite how much cerebral undercurrent academics attempt to read into Terry Southern's script, *Easy Rider* is important for one main reason: It's about getting on your bike and hitting the blacktop, a basic image that will never go out of style. Riding across the country on proceeds from their freelance drug sales, Hopper and Fonda encounter prejudice, free love, and just about everything else America has to offer. Much of *Easy Rider* is simply a serene series of rolling road shots set to late 1960s pop music. With minimal dialogue—much of it sounding like excerpts from an LSD test—this movie captured the freewheeling 60s as few other films have before or since. Often imitated, never duplicated.

The Black Angels (1970)
Director Laurence Merrick
Starring John King, Des Roberts

No collection of biker movies is complete without a few samples from the period when film studios were slapping together chopper operas faster than Harley turns out new Fat Boys. Finding one movie that epitomizes the slapdash production, chintzy budgets, and virtually non-existent plot lines is no easy job, but *Black Angels* comes pretty close. Here, we've got a film determined to offend everybody who watches it, from bikers to exotic pet owners and even people with exceedingly large afros! Centered around an ongoing gang war between two cycle mobs—the Choppers and Satan's Serpents, *Black Angels* mixes the best excesses of typical biker movies with the racial disharmony of the L.A. Riots. This epic exercise in bad acting starts with a 16-minute chase scene between two rival gang members. The chase is filmed in fast motion, which makes it all the more hilarious when it nearly wipes out a pair of nuns trying to cross the road and continues unabated except for two pit stops for sex. Riding a barn-full of stretch choppers, many featuring skyscraping exhaust pipes and five-foot sissy bars, the bikers in *Black Angels* are a motley assortment of B-movie nobodies and real members from some of Southern California's black motorcycle gangs. Just how low is the budget on this one? Well, the film's only police car has neither siren nor lights—it's actually a family sedan borrowed for several scenes. The film's editor, Clancy Symko, also plays a gang member. His dual duties help explain why, often, motorcycle engine noises and the actor's dialogue don't match what's happening on-screen. Best of all *Black Angels* contains one of the best lines in biker movies: "I'm gonna kill you, you no good egg-suckin', finger-lickin', snot pickin', scuzzy faced rat."

> "It's gettin' so a black man and a white man can't have a fight anymore without people trying to make it into a racial thing."

Index

About the Author

Mike Seate, his wife Kim, and their two cats live in Pittsburgh, Pennsylvania, where his columns on city life and pop culture can be found in *The Pittsburgh Tribune-Review*. Mike has written film and arts reviews for *In Pittsburgh Newsweekly* and has contributed hundreds of motorcycle lifestyle features to numerous magazines including *Iron-Works, LongRiders,* and *Iron Horse,* as well as England's *Classic Bike* and *Motor Cycle News.* Mike owns three motorcycles and staunchly refuses to learn to drive an automobile, preferring to spend his off-bike time reading and watching biker movies on TV.